A Will is Not Enough in Florida

2nd Edition

SIMPLE, PRACTICAL THINGS
A FLORIDA RESIDENT CAN DO TO

- ◇ PRESERVE ASSETS
- ◇ AVOID PROBATE
- ◇ AVOID GUARDIANSHIP
- ◇ PROVIDE FOR HEALTH CARE
- ◇ PROVIDE FOR THE FAMILY'S CARE

By Florida Attorney
AMELIA E. POHL

EAGLE PUBLISHING COMPANY OF BOCA

The purpose of this book is to provide the reader with an informative overview of the subject; but laws change frequently and are subject to different interpretations as courts rule on the meaning or effect of a law. This book is sold with the understanding that the publisher and the authors are not engaging in, or rendering legal, accounting, medical, psychiatric, financial planning or any other professional service. If you need legal, accounting, medical, psychiatric, financial planning or other expert advice, then you should seek the services of a licensed professional.

This book is intended for use by the consumer for his or her own benefit. If you use this book to counsel someone about the law or tax matters, then that may be considered to be an unauthorized and illegal practice.

WEB SITES: Web sites appear throughout the book. These Web sites are offered for the convenience of the reader only. Publication of these Web site addresses is not an endorsement by the authors, editors or publishers of this book.

EAGLE PUBLISHING COMPANY OF BOCA
4199 N. Dixie Highway, #2
Boca Raton, FL 33431   E-mail: info@eaglepublishing.com

Printed in the United States of America
ISBN 1-932464-01-8
Library of Congress Catalog Card Number 2004111764

A Will is Not Enough in Florida

CONTENTS

Amelia E. Pohl, Esq.

Before becoming an attorney in 1985, AMELIA E. POHL taught mathematics on both the high school and college level. During her tenure as Associate Professor of Mathematics at Prince George's Community College in Maryland, she wrote several books including:
Probability: A Set Theory Approach,
Principals of Counting
Common Stock Sense.

During her practice of law Attorney Pohl observed that many people want to reduce the high cost of legal fees by performing or assisting with their own legal transactions.

Attorney Pohl found that, with a bit of guidance, people are able to perform many legal transactions for themselves. Attorney Pohl utilizes her background as teacher, author and attorney to provide that "bit of guidance" to the general public in the form of self-help legal books that she has written. Because there is such variation in the laws from state to state, each book written by Attorney Pohl is state specific.

With the assistance of an attorney licensed to practice in the given state, Amelia Pohl is currently "translating" this book for the remaining states.

Call **EAGLE PUBLISHING COMPANY OF BOCA** at (800) 824-0823 to learn of the availability of this book for any other state.

v

Acknowledgment

We wish to thank Florida attorney GREGORY G. GAY for his editorial review of the Medicaid section of this book, namely Chapters 10 and 11. Mr. Gay received a Bachelor of Arts degree in accounting and his Juris Doctorate from Florida State University. He has a Master of Science Degree in Financial Services from the American College in 1983. He earned a Master of Arts degree in Biblical Studies from the Dallas Theological Seminary in 1998.

Mr. Gay is certified as an Elder Law attorney by the National Elder Law Foundation and also by the Florida Bar. He is also certified in Estate Planning and Probate by the Florida Bar. He is past president of the North Suncoast Estate Planning Council and also of the Tampa Bar Area Planned Giving Council. He served as Special Master for the Baker Act and Marchman Hearings in West Pasco County, Florida from 1993 through 1997.

Gregory G. Gay is the author of *The Florida Senior Legal Guide, 2nd Edition* published by the Senior Law Series, Inc. He is a columnist for the Seniority Section of the St. Petersburg Times.

Mr. Gay is married to the former Julia Juanita Stokes of Miami, Florida. They have two children. The law firm of GREGORY G. GAY, P.A. has office locations in New Port Richy, Spring Hill and Crystal River. To learn more about Mr. Gay, visit his Web site at http://www.willtrust.com.

THE DESIGN ARTIST

LUBOSH CECH designed the cover of this book. For information about Mr. Cech and the OKO Design Studio visit his Web site. http://www.okodesignstudio.com
The photograph on the cover is that of the Tampa Skyline by Photolink.

Reading the Law

Where applicable, we identified the state statute or federal statute that is the basis of the discussion. We did this as a reference, and also to encourage the reader to look at the law as it is written. Prior to the Internet the only way you could look up the law was to physically take yourself to the local courthouse law library or the law section of a public library. Today all of the state and federal statutes are literally at your finger tips. They are just a mouse click away on the Internet. To look up a statute all you need is the address of the Web site and the identifying number of the statute.

FEDERAL STATUTES
http://www4.law.cornell.edu/uscode

FLORIDA STATUTES
http://www.leg.state.fl.us

The Florida legislature organized their laws into some 985 Chapters. Each Chapter is divided into numbered sections. We will identify the statute by its Chapter and Section. For example, (FS 700.14) refers to Chapter 700, Section 14 of the Florida Statutes. To look up a statute, go to the Web site, find the title and then the section within the title. If you come across a topic that is of importance to you, you may find it both interesting and profitable to read the law as it is written.

When You Need A Lawyer

The purpose of this book is to give the reader a basic understanding of Florida law as it relates to Wills and other methods of Estate Planning. It is not intended as a substitute for legal counsel or any other kind of professional advice. If you have a legal question, you should seek the counsel of an attorney. When looking for an attorney, consider three things:

EXPERTISE, COST and PERSONALITY.

EXPERTISE

The Florida Bar has a certification program for 19 different areas of law including BUSINESS LITIGATION, CIVIL TRIAL, ELDER LAW, WILLS, TRUST AND ESTATES. To be certified by the Florida Bar as a specialist in these areas, the attorney must have practiced in that area of law for a number of years (usually 5) and pass a comprehensive Florida Bar Certification Examination.

The Florida Bar has a Statewide Referral Service. You can call them at (800) 342-8011 and ask for a referral to an attorney in your county who is experienced in the area of law that you seek. The Florida Bar has a Web site that give the name and telephone numbers of all of the Board Certified Attorneys in the state of Florida.

 THE FLORIDA BAR
http://www.flabar.org

Certification is just one of the criteria to consider. Many fine attorneys are experienced in an area of law, but the attorney have not taken the time, effort or expense to become certified as a specialist. If the attorney is not certified in the branch of law you seek, then ask how long he has practiced that type of law and what percentage of his practice is devoted to that branch of law.

One of the most reliable ways to find an attorney is through personal referral. Ask your friends, family or business acquaintances if they used an attorney for the field of law that you seek and whether they were pleased with the results. It is important to employ an attorney who is experienced in the area of law you seek. Your friend may have a wonderful Estate Planning attorney, but if you suffered an injury to your body, then you need an attorney experienced in Personal Injury.

Before employing an attorney for a job, ask how long he has practiced that type of law and what percentage of his practice is devoted to that type of law.

COST

In addition to the attorney's experience, it is important to check what it will cost in attorney's fees. When you call for an appointment ask what the attorney will charge for the initial consultation and the approximate cost for the service you seek. Ask whether there will be additional costs such as filing fees, accounting fees, expert witness fees, etc.

If the least expensive attorney is out of your price range then you can call your local county Bar Association for the telephone number of the Legal Aid office nearest you or you can call the STATEWIDE REFERRAL SERVICE at (800) 342-8011 for the telephone number of the LEGAL AID office nearest you.

The American Bar Association has a directory of Florida Legal Services Programs at the General Public Resources section of its Web site.

 THE AMERICAN BAR ASSOCIATION
http://www.abanet.org

PERSONALITY

Of equal importance to the attorney's experience and legal fees, is your relationship with the attorney. How easy was it to reach the attorney? Did you go through layers of receptionists and legal assistants before being allowed to speak to the attorney? Did the attorney promptly return your call? If you had difficulty reaching the attorney, then you can expect similar problems should you employ that attorney.

Did the attorney treat you with respect? Did the attorney treat you paternally with a "father knows best" attitude or did he treat you as an intelligent person with the ability to understand the options available to you and the ability to make your own decision based on the information provided to you?

Are you able to understand and easily communicate with the attorney? Is he speaking to you in plain English or is his explanation of the matter so full of legalese to be almost meaningless to you?

Do you find the attorney's personality to be pleasant or grating? Sometimes people rub each other the wrong way. It is like rubbing a cat the wrong way. Stroking a cat from head to tail is pleasing to the cat, but petting it in the opposite direction, no matter how well intended, causes friction. If the lawyer makes you feel annoyed or uncomfortable, then find another attorney.

It is worth the effort to take the time to interview as many attorneys as it takes to find one with the right expertise, fee schedule and personality for you.

The Organization of the Book

Many people who have a Will think they have their affairs in order, reasoning that should they die everything will go to the people named in the Will and somehow things will all be taken care of. But this is a simplistic view. There are many more things to consider.

1. What exactly will your beneficiaries inherit?
2. How will your property be transferred?
3. Can you (should you) avoid Probate?
4. Can you avoid a challenge to your Will?

The first four chapters of this book deal with these basic issues. Once you read these chapters you will have an understanding of what will happen to your property should you die, regardless of whether you do, or do not, have a Will.

The rest of the book deals with things a Will <u>cannot</u> do:

Chapter 5.   Manage your personal debt
Chapter 6.   Limit your business debt
Chapter 7.   Provide care for a minor or disabled child
Chapter 8.   Appoint someone to make your health care decisions should you be unable to do so
Chapter 9.   Appoint someone to handle your finances should you be unable to do so
Chapter 10. Help you qualify for MEDICAID should the need arise
Chapter 11. Protect your home should you need to apply for MEDICAID
Chapter 12. Help your family settle your Estate.

A Will can't do these things but you will be able to do so once you read these chapters and understand what options are available to you under Florida law.

GLOSSARY

This book is designed for the average reader. Legal terminology has been kept to a minimum. There is a glossary at the end of the book in case you come across a legal term that is not familiar to you.

FICTITIOUS NAMES AND EVENTS

The examples in this book are based loosely on actual events; however, all names are fictitious; and the events, as portrayed, are fictitious.

MALE GENDER USED

Rather than use he/she or himself/herself, for simplicity, we have used the male gender.

Your Financial Check-up 1

To understand why *A Will is Not Enough in Florida* you need to know what a Will can and cannot do. One thing a Will can do is make a gift of all you own (your *Estate*). One of the things a Will cannot do is preserve and protect your property during your lifetime. For that, you need to think about risks to your property (poor investments, theft, loss through acts of nature, etc.) and what you can do to minimize or eliminate such risk. In other words, you need an *Estate Plan* for the care and management of your property during your lifetime.

The average person may protest "I don't have an Estate; none the less an Estate Plan." But you do. Everyone who has property, has an Estate Plan. You may never have verbalized your Estate Plan, or even thought about it, but it's there none-the-less. For example, take the case of the college student purchasing his first car. If his parents bankroll the purchase, the son may offer to hold the car jointly with them. The son's Estate is his car. His Estate Plan is to hold the car jointly with his parents so that they will own the car should anything happen to him.

This may not be the best Estate Plan. Holding the car jointly with his parents may make them liable for injuries or damages should the car be involved in an accident. If the young man's parents are familiar with Florida law, they would be wise to refuse the offer and reassure their son "You can make a Will and make us the beneficiary of your car. But even if you die without a Will, we are your heirs under Florida law. Either way we will inherit the car. Just make sure to drive carefully and carry enough car insurance."

1

This is a better Estate Plan. It gives the young man maximum control over his Estate (i.e., his car) during his lifetime. He can sell the car, mortgage it, or trash it, all as he sees fit. If he follows his parent's advice, of driving carefully and purchasing sufficient insurance, his Estate will have maximum protection. If he dies without a Will, and is single and without children, under Florida's LAWS OF INTESTATE SUCCESSION, his parents will inherit his Estate. And that is just the way the son wants things at this stage of his life.

Simple situation, simple Estate Plan. But, for most of us, life isn't all that simple. We may own many items of value and have loved ones who rely on us. At some point in our lives, we need to ask:

How can I make sure that my property will be inherited by my choice of beneficiary?

How can I arrange to have my property inherited quickly and at minimum cost?

How can I achieve these goals and yet have maximum control and protection of my property during my lifetime?

We will explore the different ways to answer these questions so that you can decide on an Estate Plan that is best for you. But before doing so you need to know what property you own; i.e., how much your Estate is worth. If you are married and your spouse handles all of the finances, it may be that you have no idea of the value of your Estate.

That was the case with Kristin. She met Matt when they were both at the pinnacle of their careers, but they had no more insight into their precarious position than fireworks in a summer sky just before self-destruct.

Kristin was a model. Not the best, nor the most beautiful, but she made a comfortable living. She moved in a circle of famous models. She reflected off of their radiance, making her appear more attractive than she actually was.

Matt worked in middle management for one of those high tech companies. Like Kristin, he was not particularly gifted but he happened to be in Silicon Valley just at the time the high stakes investors were showing extraordinary, if not misguided, confidence in the industry. The good times were rolling. It never crossed Matt's mind that this would one day end. He spent the money as fast as it came in.

Kristin was impressed with the lavish gifts Matt gave to her. She, and her family, thought she made quite a catch when she announced her engagement. After the wedding she continued to model, but it took a lot of traveling and Matt resented her time away. Eventually, she agreed to stop working altogether. After all, why should she, the wife of a wealthy man, need to continue with the rigors of a model's life of diet and exercise?

Matt never told Kristin about his financial difficulties. All she knew was that he was drinking quite a bit. Her suspicion that he also was into drugs was verified when he died, suddenly, because of an overdose. Her shock and sadness turned to anger when she discovered that all he owned was mortgaged and he was heavily in debt. He even borrowed money from her family without her knowledge!

Matt's creditors took it all. The house, the boat, the Porsche, everything. If only Kristin had investigated the true state of their finances, she could have arranged to set aside the money she earned prior to her marriage and not end up as she did, a destitute widow, past her prime.

Even if you are single you may not know the value of your Estate because you have not taken the time to actually sit down and figure it out. To get maximum benefit from this book, you need to take a few minutes to determine your *Net Worth* i.e. the current value of your Estate.

ASSETS

$_____	Cash (certificates of deposit, bank accounts, etc.)
$_____	Tangible personal property (jewelry, motor vehicles, private art, stamp or coin collections, etc.)
$_____	Cash value of insurance policies
$_____	Securities (stocks, bonds, etc.)
$_____	Cash value of pension plans, IRAs, etc.
$_____	Cash value of a partnership or other business interest
$_____	Real property (residence, time share, lot, condo, cooperatives, etc.)
$_____	TOTAL VALUE OF ASSETS

It may be that you have a loan on your car or home, or any of the above items. You need to subtract away monies you owe to get the bottom line value of what you own:

LIABILITIES

$_____	Private loans
$_____	Mortgage Balance
$_____	Credit card debt
$_____	Car loan or car lease balance
$_____	TOTAL LIABILITIES

A simple subtraction gives you the value of your Estate.
ASSETS — LIABILITIES = NET WORTH

If you are married and hold all property jointly with your spouse, divide by 2 to get the value of your own Net Worth.

Your Net Worth is the value of all that you own, and that is how much your beneficiaries can inherit. Who will inherit your property depends on how your property is *titled* (held or owned).

There are three basic ways to title property:
- ⇨ in *your name only*　- or -
- ⇨ *jointly* with another　- or -
- ⇨ *in trust for* another.

The way your property is titled determines who will inherit that property:

> Property held in your **name only** will be inherited by the beneficiaries named in your Will.
> If you have no Will, the property will go to your heirs according to Florida's Laws of Intestate Succession.
>
> Property you hold **jointly** will go to the surviving joint owner(s) of that property.
>
> Property held in **Trust** will go to those you name as the beneficiary of the Trust.
>
> **NOTE** ⇨ If you are married, your spouse may have rights in your property, regardless of the way your property is titled.

We will examine each of these types of ownership in detail so that you can give yourself an Estate Planning check-up, i.e., you can check whether the way you are currently holding your property accomplishes your Estate Planning goals.

MINE, ALL MINE

There's much to be said about holding property in your name only and not jointly or in trust for another. There's maximum control. You can sell it, trade it, mortgage it, with no one to account to, or ask "may I?" How you protect your assets depends on how much security you require. Again, it's all up to you.

As discussed, there are three things to consider when setting up an Estate Plan:

CONTROL — How to control and protect your Estate during your lifetime.

BENEFICIARY — How to be sure your Estate goes to the beneficiary of your choice.

COST — How to transfer your Estate to your beneficiaries at lowest cost.

Holding all of your property in your name only should give you maximum control and protection; but such an Estate Plan may present problems with the cost of transferring your property upon your death. More than likely it will take some sort of court procedure to transfer that property once you die. The name of the court procedure is *Probate*. In Florida, Probate is conducted in the Probate Division of the County Court (FS 26.012). We will refer to the court that handles Probate as the *Probate Court*. We will refer to property that is transferred to your beneficiary by means of a Probate procedure as your *Probate Estate*, and the person appointed by the Court to settle the Estate as your *Personal Representative*.

Probate can be expensive, so if you keep all of your property in your name only there could be a significant cost to transfer your property to the beneficiary of your Estate.

Holding property in your name should not create a problem with having your choice of beneficiary inherit your Estate, provided you have a valid Will. But if you die *intestate* (without a Will) the Probate Court will use Florida's Laws of Intestate Succession to determine who gets your property. Of course it could be that the beneficiaries of your Estate under the Laws of Intestate Succession are exactly who you would have wanted, had you taken the time to prepare a Will. To help you determine if this is the case, we will take a few pages to explain the Law. Those who have a Will might be tempted to skip over the section, but, this information is good to know in the event someone in your family dies in Florida without a Will. Once you read this section you will know whether you have a right to inherit their property.

THE FAMILY'S RIGHT TO INHERIT

The state of Florida recognizes the right of the family to inherit property left by the *decedent* (the person who died); so the Laws of Intestate Succession cover all possible relationships beginning with the surviving spouse. In order for the spouse to inherit property under the Laws of Intestate Succession, the state of Florida needs to recognize the union as a valid marriage.

Who Is Your Spouse?

In this era of people challenging the concept of the family unit, those of a philosophical bent may ponder the meaning of marriage. Is it a union of two people in the eyes of God? Is it even a union? Maybe it is just a contract between two people. The state of Florida does not concern itself with such things. If a person dies without a Will, then the state will distribute the property according to the laws of Florida; and the laws of Florida determine whether two people are married.

BEING MARRIED IN FLORIDA

To be married in Florida means that a man and a woman have obtained a license to marry from the state, solemnized the marriage by a state or religious ceremony, and then cohabited together as man and wife. Parental consent to marry is required for anyone under 18 but over 16. No one under 16 may marry without Court permission. The Court may issue a license to marry with or without parental consent provided the girl is pregnant or has a child (FS 741.04, 741.0405).

Florida law specifically prohibits the marriage of people who are:

☒ currently married.

Anyone who knows he is married and then deliberately commits bigamy can be convicted of a felony of the third degree (FS 826.01).

☒ related to each other as follows:
⇨ **ancestors** (parent, grandparents, etc.) or **descendants** (child, grandchild, etc.) of each other;
⇨ aunt and nephew or uncle and niece;
⇨ brother and sister (FS 741.21)

Florida law does not bar marriages between cousins.

☒ of the same sex.

Vermont was the first state to recognize a same sex marriage, which they refer to as a "civil union." Several other states, including Florida, have passed statutes, specifically denying marital status to couples of the same gender, regardless of whether that marriage is valid in any other state or country (FS 741.212).

THE COMMON LAW MARRIAGE

A common law marriage is one that has not been solemnized by ceremony. It is more than just living together. The couple must agree to live together as man and wife, and then publicly hold themselves out as being married; i.e., tell friends and family that they are married. Many states no longer recognize a common law marriage as being valid, and have passed laws to that effect. The state of Florida does not recognize a common law marriage that was entered into in the state of Florida after January 1, 1968 (FS 741.211).

Florida respects the laws of other states, so even though common law marriages are no longer valid in Florida, Courts have ruled that they will recognize a common law marriage if it is valid in the state where the couple entered into the marriage (*In Re Estate of Goldfarb*, 502 So.2d 963 (Fla.App. 3 Dist. 1987)).

Now that you know whether the State of Florida considers you to be married, the next question is whether the state recognizes anyone as your descendant.

Who Is Your Child?

Medical technology has made important contributions to solving the problem of infertility. There are all sorts of solutions, from hormone therapy, to sperm banks that provide donations anonymously, to frozen sperm and/or ova to be thawed and used at a later date, to women who become a surrogate or gestational mother. Solving a set of medical problems has opened the door to a new set of legal problems. Used to be, the only question was "Who's the father?"

Now it could well be "Who's the mother? "

To answer these questions, the State of Florida has passed laws to legally establish the parentage of children whose conception was assisted by medical technology. We will examine the law as it relates to the right of the child to inherit property.

FROZEN SPERM AND THE AFTERBORN CHILD

Under Florida law a child conceived prior to death and born to the surviving spouse after the death, has the same right to inherit as any other natural child of the decedent (FS 732.106). But suppose the child was conceived after death? That question is becoming more of an issue as couples are freezing egg cells, sperm, and pre-embryo (fertilized cells) for use at a later date. Often the purpose of the procedure is to protect the cell from damage during cancer treatments. If the treatment is unsuccessful, the surviving parent may decide to go ahead with the pregnancy using the frozen pre-embryo.

This raises issues of whether the surviving parent has the right to use these reproductive cells without the written consent of the deceased donor; and whether a child born of such procedure is entitled to inherit from the deceased donor.

This inheritance issue has important consequences, not only on the state level but on the federal level as well. A minor child who has lost a parent is entitled to Social Security benefits, but those benefits are based on the state's Laws of Intestate Succession. Section 216 of the Social Security Act provides "a child's insurance benefits can be paid to a child who could inherit under the State's intestate laws." Specifically, a child cannot receive Social Security benefits, unless the child is entitled to inherit under the state's Laws of Intestate Succession.

This issue was brought before the Superior Court in New Jersey. The Court ruled that a child conceived and born after the death of a parent can inherit under New Jersey's Laws of Intestate Succession (*In Re Estate of Kolacy*, 322 N.J.Super. 593 (2000)).

The Florida legislature passed a law with the opposite result. Florida Statute 742.17 requires the physician who performs the procedure to enter into a written agreement with the intended parents. The agreement must state what is to be done with the reproductive cell in the event of a divorce or the death of one of the donors. Regardless of what the parties agree to, if one of the donors dies before the cell is transferred to a woman's body, under statute 742.17, the child cannot inherit property from the deceased donor under Florida's Laws of Intestate Succession.

Still another legal issue raised because of modern technology is the question of the rights of the Surrogate (gestational) mother as opposed to the rights of the biological parent who donates sperm or egg cell to the Surrogate mother under a Surrogate Parenting Contract.

THE SURROGATE PARENTING CONTRACT

A Surrogate Parenting Contract is an agreement, usually between a married couple (the intended parents) and a woman (the gestational or Surrogate mother), in which the woman agrees to be the birth mother of a child conceived with the sperm of the husband, or the egg cell of the wife, or the embryo of the married couple, or none of these. This means that the husband or wife might be, but is not necessarily, the biological parent of the child born of the Surrogate mother.

Some states such as New York and Michigan consider Surrogate Parenting Contracts as being against public policy and have laws prohibiting such contracts. Florida law allows a couple to contract with a woman to have their baby, provided the parties conform to the law of the state. In particular, Florida law strictly prohibits any fee to be paid or charged to arrange or participate in such arrangement. The law does allow the intended parents to pay for medical care and living expenses of the Surrogate mother (FS 63.212).

Florida statute 742.15 requires that the Surrogate mother be at least 18 years of age and the couple be unable to bear their own child for valid medical reasons. The contract must provide that once the child is born, the Surrogate mother will give up all rights to the child's biological parent(s). The intended parents agree to raise the child and be fully responsible for its care, regardless of any impairment that the child may suffer.

Within 3 days after the child's birth, the couple need to *petition* (ask) the Court to affirm their parent status; i.e., to rule that they are the parents of the child.

If the petition is granted the Court will order the Department of Health to issue a new birth certificate naming the intended parents as the child's parents and requiring the Department of Health to seal the original birth certificate (FS 742.16).

THE PREPLANNED ADOPTION AGREEMENT

A couple may enter into a Preplanned Adoption Agreement with a woman (the *Volunteer Mother*) to adopt a child born to that woman. As with the Surrogate Parenting contract, the Volunteer Mother must be at least 18 years of age; and no money may be paid other than for the medical and living expenses of the Volunteer Mother. Unlike the Surrogate mother, the Volunteer mother must agree that she is fully responsible to care for the child in the event that the intended parents decide to terminate the agreement prior to the adoption. Once the child is born the Volunteer Mother has 7 days to change her mind about going through with the adoption. If all of the parties decide to honor the Preplanned Adoption Agreement, they still need to go through a regular adoption procedure, with the final decision to allow the adoption in the hands of the Court (FS 63.212).

THE ADOPTED CHILD

An adopted person has the same right to inherit property under Florida's Laws of Intestate Success from his adoptive parents as does a natural child. The adopted child has no right to inherit from his natural parents, with the exception of the natural parent who is married to the adoptive parent. For example, if a child loses a parent and is later adopted by a step-parent, the child has the right to inherit from his natural parents and from his adoptive parent as well (FS 63.172).

In the absence of a Surrogate or Preplanned Adoption Agreement, a sperm or egg cell donor gives up all rights to the child born as a result of the donation. The husband of a child born to a married woman by means of artificial insemination is considered to be child's father, provided he gave his written consent for the procedure.

A child born to a married couple using any other form of assisted conception has the same rights as a child conceived the old fashioned way. It is presumed that the husband consented to the assisted conception procedure. If that is not the case, and he is not the father of the child, he can ask the court to terminate his parental rights and responsibilities. If the husband is successful, the child will not be able to inherit from the husband, nor from his family (FS 742.11, 742.14).

THE NON-MARITAL CHILD

A child born out of wedlock has the same rights to inherit from his/her natural father as does one born in wedlock, provided any one of the following are true:

☑ He and the mother participated in a marriage ceremony before or after the birth, even though the marriage is not valid for some reason.

☑ The father acknowledges his paternity in writing.

☑ The father's paternity is established by a Court either before or after his death (FS 732.108).

Now that we know who the state of Florida considers to be your spouse, and who is considered your child, we can determine how much of your Probate Estate they each are entitled to inherit under Florida's Laws of Intestate Succession.

Should you die with property titled in your name only, and without a Will, then the state of Florida provides one for you in the form of the Laws of Intestate Succession (FS 732.101). Once your debts, funeral expenses, and the cost of the Probate procedure are paid, whatever is left (your net Probate Estate) is distributed as follows:

◇ SINGLE, WITH DESCENDANT

If you are not married and have children, all of whom survive you, then they will inherit your net Probate Estate in equal shares, *per stirpes*; meaning that if a child dies before you do, the share intended for that child goes to his descendants. If the child dies without descendants, then the remaining children inherit the net Probate Estate (FS 732.103).

◇ MARRIED, NO DESCENDANT

If you are married with no surviving *lineal descendants* (child, grandchild, great-grandchild, etc.), all of your net Probate Estate goes to your surviving spouse.

◇ MARRIED, WITH DESCENDANT

If you are married, and all of your descendants are also those of your surviving spouse, your spouse inherits the first $60,000 and half of the remainder of the net Probate Estate. Your children inherit the other half, in equal shares, per stirpes. If you have a descendant who is not that of your surviving spouse, then your surviving spouse takes half of the net Probate Estate and your descendants take the other half in equal shares, per stirpes (FS 732.102).

✧ NO CHILD, NO SPOUSE

If you have no spouse or descendant, then your Probate Estate is divided equally between your parents. If only one of your parents is alive, then all of your Probate Estate goes to that parent. If neither parent is alive, then the Estate goes to your brothers and sisters in equal shares, per stirpes.

If you have half-blood siblings they inherit half the amount inherited by full blooded siblings. For example, if you are survived by one brother with the same set of parents, and another brother with the same father and a different mother, then the full blooded brother inherits two-thirds of your net Probate Estate and the half-blooded brother inherits one-third of your Estate (FS 732.108).

If you have no brothers, sisters, nephews or nieces, your Probate Estate is divided with half going to your maternal grandparents (or to the survivor of them) and the other half to your paternal grandparents (or the survivor of them). If neither maternal grandparent survives you, then their half goes to their descendants in equal shares, per stirpes; i.e., to your aunts and uncles or to the descendants of a deceased aunt or uncle (i.e., your cousins).

The other half going to your next of kin on your father's side in the same manner. If there are next of kin on one side of the family only, then the entire Probate Estate is distributed to your next of kin on that side of your family (FS 732.103).

FLORIDA: HEIR OF LAST RESORT

In Florida, property that is either unclaimed or abandoned, goes to the state, so if you die without a Will and you have absolutely no one who can inherit your property under the Laws of Intestate Succession, then the state of Florida will "inherit" your Probate Estate. Your net Probate Estate will be paid to the Treasurer of the state, who will deposit it into the State School Fund (FS 732.107).

 ## IT ISN'T ALL THAT SIMPLE

The explanation in this book of the Laws of Intestate Succession is abridged. Even though you may now know more about Florida's Intestate Succession than you ever wanted to know, there is much more to the law. For example, if you have absolutely no living blood relatives, but you have a deceased spouse, your Intestate property will go to the relatives of your deceased spouse, as determined by Florida's Laws of Intestate Succession (FL 732.103).

But why chance having your property go to someone you may not even know? Best to prepare a Will and have your property inherited by the person of your choice.

THE COST OF PROBATE

Holding property in your name only gives you maximum control and protection during your lifetime. If you do not like the way your property will be distributed should you die without a Will, then you can control who inherits your property by preparing a Will. But there is still the question of what it will cost to transfer your Estate to your beneficiaries. In all probability, a Probate procedure will be necessary. How much of your Estate will need to be spent to Probate your Estate?

THE SMALL PROBATE ESTATE

There is no need to be concerned about the cost of Probate, if all you leave is enough to pay for your funeral and medical bills for the last 60 days of your illness, a motor vehicle and personal property worth no more than $10,000. Your beneficiary can write a letter to the Judge, explaining who is entitled to inherit your Estate either under your Will or according to the Laws of Intestate Succession; how much property is in the Probate Estate; and what bills need to be paid. The Judge will determine whether the information is true and if so, he will send a letter to whomever has possession of the property, authorizing the bank, securities broker, or other person in possession of the property, to transfer that property to the beneficiary of your Estate (FS 732.402, 735.301).

THE SUMMARY ADMINISTRATION

There is a shortened Probate procedure for Estates worth $75,000, or less. The Personal Representative can pay all bills, and then ask the Court to allow him to distribute what is left to the beneficiaries. This is called a *Summary Administration* because it can be done quickly, concisely and with little formality. If no beneficiary or creditor objects, the Court will grant the request; and that's all there is to the Probate procedure (FS 735.201, 735.203).

Although a Summary Administration can be completed quickly, a Personal Representative still needs to be appointed and he will need the services of an attorney to file the necessary documents. As we will see in the next few pages, even for an Estate as small as $75,000, the Personal Representative is entitled to a fee of $2,250 and his attorney is entitled to a fee of $3,000. And Summary Administration is not available if:

☒ someone challenges the Will

☒ there is a dispute about who has the right to inherit the Estate

☒ there is an argument about what each beneficiary should receive;

☒ there is a disagreement about whether a bill should be paid

☒ there is not enough money in the Estate to pay all the bills.

Should any of these issues arise, there will need to be a full Probate procedure, and the Personal Representative and attorney fees might be significantly greater than the above figures.

THE FORMAL PROBATE ADMINISTRATION

There will need to be a formal Probate procedure if you leave property in your name only worth more than $75,000. If you leave a valid Will naming someone to serve as your Personal Representative, the Court will appoint that person for the job and issue *Letters of Administration* i.e., a document giving your Personal Representative authority to settle your Estate (FS 731.201).

The formal Probate procedure is involved and time consuming; not to mention, expensive. Administration of the Estate can take anywhere from several months to more than a year, depending on the size and complexity of the Estate. Your Personal Representative must take possession of your Probate Estate and file an inventory with the Court. He might need to employ an appraiser to evaluate the property (FS 733.604).

Your Personal Representative must notify all of your creditors that they have a right to come forward and file a *claim* (i.e. a demand for payment) for monies that you may owe. As soon as the Personal Representative is appointed, he will publish notice to creditors in the newspaper for two consecutive weeks. The notice will state that creditors have 3 months from the first date of publication date of the order to come forward and present their claims (FS 733.2121, 733.702).

It is the responsibility of the Personal Representative to see that the Probate procedure is conducted properly. If the Personal Representative makes a mistake then he may be responsible to pay for that mistake. For example, if he pays a debt that did not need to be paid — or if he transfers property to the beneficiaries too quickly and there were still taxes due on the Estate, then he may be responsible to pay for such error (FS 198.23).

To avoid mistakes, the Personal Representative needs to employ an attorney to guide him through the process. It then becomes the attorney's job to see to it that the Estate is administered according to Florida law and without any liability to the Personal Representative.

PERSONAL REPRESENTATIVE'S FEES

The Personal Representative is entitled to compensation for his efforts. Florida statute has a schedule of reasonable fees for the Personal Representative based on the value of the Probate Estate:

    3% of the first million dollars

  2.5% of amounts over $1,000,000 and up to $5,000,000

    2% of amounts over $5,000,000 and up to $10,000

  1.5% of amounts over ten million dollars.

Compensation for the Personal Representative is subject to the Court's approval. When awarding fees the Court can take into account extraordinary or unusual services performed by the Personal Representative. For example, additional compensation can be awarded for:

    ⇨   selling real or personal property

    ⇨   participating in a proceeding involving the adjustment of Estate taxes

    ⇨   conducting a law suit on behalf of or against the decedent's Estate

    ⇨   carrying on the decedent's business (FS 733.617)

ATTORNEY FEES

The attorney for the Personal Representative has the right to receive fees for his services and those fees are a proper charge to your Probate Estate. Florida statute 733.6171 contains a schedule of attorney's fees. It is based on the value of the Probate Estate:

$1,500 for Estates of $40,000 or less   - plus -
$750 for Estates greater than $40,000
    but less than $70,000   - plus -
$750 for Estates greater than $70,000
    but less than $100,000   - plus -
3% on the next $900,000, then
2.5% of amounts above 1 million but less than 3 million
2% of amounts over 3 million but less than 5 million
1.5% of amounts over 5 million but less than 10 million
1% of amounts over 10 million dollars

If the attorney prepares the federal Estate Tax return, the attorney is entitled to percentage of the value of the gross Estate, which according to the statue is:

0.5% for Estates up to 10 million dollars - plus -
0.25% of amounts over 10 million dollars.

The above fee schedule is for "ordinary" services. The attorney is entitled to additional compensation for any "extraordinary" service. Florida statute 733.6171 lists 11 items in addition to preparing the federal Estate Tax return. The list includes disputes of any kind (Will disputes, fees disputes, claim disputes, etc.). The sale, lease or purchase of real property; legal advice relating to the continuation of the decedent's business during the Probate procedure, any kind of tax advice, are also considered "extraordinary" services, that may entitle the attorney to additional compensation.

THE COST OF A FULL PROBATE PROCEDURE

The Personal Representative and attorney's fees are significant charges to the Probate Estate; but they are not the only charges against the Estate. A Probate procedure can incur some or all of the following expenses:

$$ Court fees to file the Probate procedure

$$ The cost of a bond that the Court may order for the protection of your Probate Estate

$$ The cost of notifying your creditors which may include publishing notice, or mailing notice to them by registered or certified mail

$$ The cost of an appraisal

$$ Accounting fees to prepare an inventory, and account for monies spent during the Probate procedure

$$ The cost of transferring property to the proper beneficiary; i.e., recording fees, broker fees to sell securities or real estate

Once the above costs, Personal Representative fees, attorney fees, taxes and all valid claims are paid, the Personal Representative will distribute whatever is left to the proper beneficiary and then close the Estate. However, under Florida law, he is not required to make any distribution until at least 5 months have passed from the date of his appointment (FS 733.801).

You may be thinking that Probate is a good thing to avoid. Why should your Personal Representative go through all that effort to settle your Estate? Why should your beneficiaries wait months or maybe years, and pay all these fees to inherit your Estate? There are ways to arrange your Estate so that your beneficiaries can immediately inherit your Estate without incurring unnecessary costs. In the next two chapters we will examine each of these methods in detail.

Is Probate Necessary? 2

Many people think that only wealthy people need to make plans to avoid Probate, yet each year, heirs of relatively modest estates, spend thousands of dollars to settle an Estate. A bit of Estate Planning could have eliminated most, if not all, of the cost (and hassle) suffered by those families.

If you have a small Estate and only one or two beneficiaries, then it is not all that difficult to arrange your finances to eliminate the need for Probate altogether. All you need do is title your property so that it automatically goes to your beneficiaries. There are any ways to arrange your finances to achieve this result. The most common method is to hold property jointly with another. Such an arrangement is the Estate Plan of choice for most married couples. Husband and wife often hold all of their property jointly, so that the surviving spouse has complete and immediate access to their property without any need for Probate.

Holding property jointly may not be the most desirable method for the single person, or for the surviving spouse who is now single. There are other ways to ensure that your property is inherited quickly and without cost to your heirs. In this chapter, we explore the pros and cons of different methods of holding property so that it can be transferred without the need for Probate.

PROPERTY OWNED JOINTLY

Bank accounts, securities, motor vehicles, real property can all be owned by two or more people. If one of the owners dies, then the survivor(s) continue to own their share of the property. Who owns the share belonging to the decedent depends on Florida law and how ownership of the property was set up.

THE JOINT BANK ACCOUNT

When a bank account is opened in two or more names, each depositor is given a statement of the terms and conditions of the account. The statement will say whether each owner has authority to make a withdrawal, or whether two signatures are necessary. The statement will also say whether there are *rights of survivorship*. Unless the agreement with the bank states differently, it is presumed that a Joint Account has rights of survivorship (FS 655.78, 655.79).

Once an owner of a Joint Account dies, the surviving owner is free to withdraw all of the monies from the account without the need to go through any Probate procedure to get that money. You can arrange to have all of your bank accounts set up so that should you die, the money goes directly to a beneficiary, and without the need to go through a Probate procedure to get that money. For example, suppose all you own is a bank account and you want whatever you have in the account to go to your child should you die, and without any responsibility to pay for your debts from that account. You might think that a simple solution is to make your child joint owner of the account, but first consider the problems associated with a joint account.

⊠ OVERREACHING

Making your child a joint owner of the account gives the child free access to the account. Monies may be withdrawn without your knowledge or authorization. You may be thinking that couldn't happen because you would immediately know of the withdrawal, and you could force the child to return the money. That may be true when you are healthy and alert. But in this ever aging society, it is likely that you will live to an advanced age and not be as aware as you are today. And if you have two children and decided to hold your account jointly with them, then there may be a problem with how the funds are distributed should you die.

That was the case with Amanda. All she had when her husband died, was a bank account worth $50,000. She wanted to be sure that the money would go to her two sons, Robert and Leon, without the need for Probate. She went to the bank with her two sons and opened a new survivorship account with all three names on the account as joint owners.

Several years passed without incident. As Amanda aged, her health began to fail, and she became more and more dependent on Robert. She needed his assistance to take her to the doctor, to do her shopping, and of course take care of her finances. Robert had a wife and two children, so it was hard for him to care for his family and his mother as well. Leon was single, yet he never seemed to have the time to help care for his mother. And Robert resented that.

Finally, Amanda died.

After the funeral, Leon asked Robert about the bank account "Didn't Mom have a joint account in our names?"

"Yeah, but I closed it out. There was only a few thousand left, and I used it for her funeral."

Leon thought it strange that all of the money was gone, so he went to the bank and asked to see the record of withdrawals. He found that over the last two years Robert had written several large checks to himself. There was only $7,000 left in the account when Robert closed it out, within a week of her death.

Leon fumed for several weeks before he brought up the subject. Robert's face flushed when Leon asked about the money. Leon did not know if it was from anger or embarrassment. He soon learned that it was both when Robert asked "Where were you for the past two years? You never once helped. Did you know she became incontinent at the end? Who cleaned up? Not you. She blessed me every day. She often said she would have been dead long ago if it wasn't for me. She wanted me to have that money!"

"Mom never said anything to me about wanting you to have the money. She never asked for my help and neither did you. It isn't right for you to throw this up to me now."

The boys never spoke of the money again. But then there were few times that they ever spoke to each other after that.

Overreaching isn't the only problem with a joint account, there is also the problem of liability.

⊠ POTENTIAL LIABILITY

If you hold a bank account jointly with your adult child and that child is sued or gets a divorce, then the child may need to disclose his ownership of the joint account. In such a case, you may find yourself spending money to prove that the account was established for convenience only and that all of the money in that account really belongs to you.

Because of these inherent problems, you might want to hold the funds so that your beneficiary does not have access to the monies unless you die while the account is open. You can do so by opening a *Beneficiary Account*.

THE BENEFICIARY ACCOUNT

As explained, the terms of a bank account are established when a bank account is opened. Your agreement gives directions about who can access your account during your lifetime, but it can also give directions about what to do with the account should you die. If you hold the account in your name only and do not give any such directions, then should you die while the account is open, the monies in your account will become part of your Probate Estate and will be distributed in the same way as any other item that you hold in your name only.

One way to avoid Probate of the account yet retain full control of the account during your lifetime, is to name one or more persons to be the beneficiary of your account. There are two forms of beneficiary account. Your contract with the bank can direct the bank to hold your account *In Trust For* ("ITF") one or more beneficiaries that you name. An In-Trust-For Account is also known as a *Totten Trust*. (FS 655.82, 655.825).

Another type of beneficiary account is an account that directs the bank to **Pay On Death** ("POD") all of the money in the account to one or more beneficiaries that you name (FS 655.82, 655.825).

With both the In Trust For and Pay On Death Account, unless your contract with the bank says differently:

⇨ The beneficiary does not have access to the account during your lifetime.

⇨ You, as the owner of the account, have complete control over the account. You can add to it or close it or change beneficiaries without asking anyone's permission to do so.

⇨ Should your beneficiary die before you do, then the account will become part of your Probate Estate.

If you are married, you may want to hold the account jointly with your spouse with directions to the bank to give the funds to one or more beneficiaries that you name. For example, if an account is titled as:

ELDON CONNORS and LORRAINE CONNORS, JT TEN
POD ELDON CONNORS, JR. AND FRED CONNORS

Then unless the contract with the bank says differently:

⇨ The children (Eldon, Jr. and Fred) have no right to the account during the lifetime of their parents.

⇨ If either Eldon or Lorraine dies, the surviving party owns the account, and is free to close the account or change the beneficiary of the account.

⇨ Once Eldon and Lorraine are deceased, their sons share the money in the account equally. If one son should die before his parents, the surviving son will inherit the account (FS 655.81, 655.82).

THE TRANSFER ON DEATH SECURITY

The Florida law for securities is similar to the statute for banks. You can instruct the holder of the security to Pay On Death or to **TRANSFER ON DEATH ("TOD")** to a named beneficiary. As with the Pay On Death account, the Transfer On Death designation has no effect on the ownership of the security until the owner of the security dies. The security can be held jointly with another with instructions that once both owners of the security die, the security is to be transferred to a named beneficiary (FS 711.51, 711.505, 711.506).

This is a convenient way of owning a security for the married couple who want a child to inherit the security without going through a Probate procedure. For example, a securities account can be held as follows:

TIM REILLY, OLIVIA REILLY, JT TEN TOD
STUART REILLY, LDPS

which is short-hand for:

"TIM REILLY and OLIVIA REILLY own this security jointly. Upon the death of the surviving Joint Tenant, transfer this security to STUART REILLY. If STUART is deceased, then transfer this security to his lineal descendants, per stirpes."

If your Estate consists of bank accounts and/or securities only, and you want all of your property to go to one or two beneficiaries without the need for Probate, but with maximum control and protection of your funds during your lifetime, then holding your property in any of these beneficiary forms: "In Trust For"
            "Pay On Death"
            "Transfer On Death"
should accomplish your goal.

REAL PROPERTY OWNED JOINTLY

If you own real property together with another, then who will own the property upon your death depends on how the current owner is identified on the face of the deed. The top paragraph of the deed should identify the person who transferred the property to you as the "party of the first part" or the "Grantor." The person to whom the property was transferred is called the "party of the second part" or the "Grantee" (FS 689.02). The deed might read something like:

> This indenture, made this day, March 15, 2002, between ROBERT TRAYNOR, a single man, whose address is 123 Main Street, Miami, county of Dade, state of Florida
> party of the first part,
> and ALFRED CODY and ROBERT CODY
> as, JOINT TENANTS WITH RIGHT OF SURVIVOR
> party of the second part, . . .

Should either Alfred or Robert die, the survivor will own the property 100% Nothing need be done to establish that ownership, but the name of the deceased joint owner remains on the deed. The surviving owner can record the decedent's death certificate so that anyone who examines the title to the property will know that the survivor is now the sole owner of the property.

▤ DEED HELD AS TENANTS IN COMMON

You might have a deed that names you and another person as Grantee, followed by TENANTS IN COMMON. Should you die, your share of the property will go to whomever you named as beneficiary of that share in your Will. If you die without a Will, Florida Laws of Intestate Succession determine who inherits the property.

If your deed names you and another as Grantee, but does not say that you are Tenants In Common or if the deed says you are Joint Tenants, but does not say there is a Right of Survivorship, then under Florida law, you own the property as a Tenant In Common (FS 689.15).

▤ DEED HELD AS HUSBAND AND WIFE

If a married couple hold property as follows:
TODD AMES AND SUSAN AMES, husband and wife
- or -
TODD AMES AND SUSAN AMES, his wife
- or -
TODD AMES AND SUSAN AMES, TENANTS BY THE ENTIRETY

Property held as Tenants By The Entirety is similar to a joint tenancy in that when one spouse dies, the surviving spouse owns the property 100%. The difference between a Joint Tenancy and a Tenancy By The Entirety, is that each Joint Tenant owns an equal share of the property; however, with a Tenancy By The Entirety, each partner is considered to own the property 100% both before and after the death of his partner.

🗐 DEED WITH A LIFE ESTATE

A *Life Estate* interest in real property means that the person who owns the Life Estate has the right to live in that property until he/she dies. You can identify a Life Estate interest by examining the face of the deed. If somewhere on the face of the deed you see the phrase RESERVING A LIFE ESTATE, the Grantee cannot take possession of the property until the owner of the Life Estate dies. For example, suppose the granting paragraph of the deed reads:

This indenture, made this day, January 15, 2002, between ROSE CAVALLO, a single woman, . . . party of the first part, hereinafter referred to as Grantor covenants and grants to, SALVATORE CAVALLO, party of the second part, hereinafter referred to as the Grantee

RESERVING A LIFE ESTATE TO ROSE CAVALLO
. . .

Rose is the owner of the Life Estate. Salvatore is the owner of the *Remainder Interest*. Rose has the right to occupy the premises during her lifetime or to rent it out and receive the income from the property. During Rose's lifetime, Salvatore has no right to the possession of, or the income from, the property. Once Rose dies, Salvatore will own the property and is free to take possession of the property and to lease, sell or transfer it, as he sees fit.

If you are an owner of the Life Estate interest, upon your death, no Probate procedure will be necessary to transfer the property to the owner of the Remainder Interest.

THE INVISIBLE LIFE ESTATE

If your principal residence (i.e., your **homestead**) is in the state of Florida, and you are married and own that home in your name only, your surviving spouse has a Life Estate in your home. The Remainder Interest goes to your children in equal shares, per stirpes.

This means that even though you may have owned the property before your marriage, and even though the deed is in your name only, your spouse has the right to live out his/her life in your home. Once your spouse is deceased, your children will inherit the property, in equal shares, per stirpes.

If you have no surviving lineal descendants, then your spouse inherits your homestead (FS 732.201, 732.401, Florida Constitution Article X, Section 4(c)).

Florida statute 732.702 allows a spouse to **waive** (give up) the Life Estate interest. If there is a properly executed pre-nuptial or post-nuptial agreement that waives the Life Estate interest, then your surviving spouse does not have any right to the homestead.

No Probate procedure is necessary if you own property in Florida as:

⇨ the owner of a Life Estate   - or -

⇨ a Tenant By The Entirety   - or -

⇨ a Joint Tenant with Right of Survivorship.

As explained, In each of these cases, the surviving owner will own the property 100%, however your name remains on the deed. The Florida office of Vital Statistics is responsible to issue the death certificate, but not to publish it or make it part of the public record. If the surviving owner wishes to transfer the property, he will need to produce a certified copy of the death certificate. If there is a Probate procedure for other property you own, then a title search at the time of transfer will reveal that a Probate procedure was conducted. If no Probate is necessary, the surviving owner can have a certified copy of the death certificate recorded with the Clerk of the Circuit Court in the county where the property is located (FS 28.222).

For a married decedent, it is also a good idea to have the attorney for the surviving spouse prepare AFFIDAVIT OF CONTINUOUS MARRIAGE. An *Affidavit* is a statement of fact sworn to before a Notary Public. When the Affidavit is recorded, with the Clerk of the Circuit Court, anyone examining title to property owned by the couple will know that the couple was married at the time of death, and that the survivor is entitled to all of the rights of a surviving spouse under Florida law.

WHEN PROBATE IS NECESSARY

If you own Florida property in your name only, or as a Tenant In Common, it will take a Probate procedure to transfer property to your intended beneficiary. As explained in Chapter 1, the type of Probate procedure will depend on the size of your Estate.

OUT OF STATE PROPERTY

This chapter relates only to real property you own in Florida. If you own property in another state or country, the laws of that state or country determine who has the right to inherit property in that state. Whether or not there are rights of survivorship depend on the laws of that state. In Florida, property held as Joint Tenants means that there are rights of survivorship. But another states may require that the deed specifically state that there are Rights Of Survivorship. In such states, a deed held as Joint Tenants, and no stated Right of Survivorship, is the same as a Tenancy In Common. If you own out of state property jointly with another, it is important that you check with an attorney in that state to be sure that your share of the property will go to the person of your choice.

If you are married, and own property in your name only, you need to be aware that your spouse may have rights in that property. That is the case in Community property states. In other states, a surviving spouse may have Dower rights or other statutory rights. In the next chapter, we will discuss the statutory rights of a surviving spouse in real property located in Florida. If you are married and own property in another state, you need to determine the rights of your spouse in that state as well. Still another concern is whether a Probate procedure will be necessary to transfer out of state property that you own to your beneficiary.

TRANSFERRING OUT OF STATE PROPERTY

Each state is in charge of the way real property located in that state is transferred. Most state laws are similar to Florida, namely, property you hold as a Joint Tenant with Right of Survivorship or property in which you hold a Life Estate interest are transferred without the need for Probate. Property you own as a Tenant In Common or in your name only may require a Probate procedure in order to transfer the property to your beneficiary.

If you own property in your name only in this state and in another state, upon your death it may be necessary to have a Probate proceeding in Florida, and an *ancillary* (secondary) Probate proceeding in the state where the property is located. This can double the cost of Probate.

Still another problem with out of state property is the matter of taxes. Many states have an income tax. Some have an inheritance or transfer tax. Estate taxes may be due in the state where the property is located as well as in Florida. It may be necessary to file a tax return in two states. In addition to increased taxes, this can significantly increase the cost of accounting fees.

If you own property in another state, it is important to consult with an attorney to learn the answers to all of these questions, namely:

Who will inherit my property under the laws of the state where it is located?

Will a Probate procedure be necessary to transfer that property to my beneficiaries?

What taxes will need to be paid in that state?

If you find that Probate will be necessary to transfer real property that you own in Florida or elsewhere, you may decide that the cost of Probate is too expensive. You may be tempted to go for the quick fix of having the deed to the property changed so that you are joint owners with the intended beneficiary of the property; or you may decide to transfer the property to your intended beneficiary and keep a Life Estate for yourself.

This will avoid Probate, but it may not be the best Estate Plan because you will not have maximum control over the property during your lifetime. If you hold real property as a Joint Tenant or as a Life Tenant, you will not be able to sell that property during your lifetime without getting permission from your beneficiary. And if the beneficiary gives permission and the property is sold, the beneficiary will have the legal right to share in the proceeds of the sale.

You may be thinking "I can make my son joint owner of my home and avoid any need for Probate. I trust him to do what I want with the property. If I decide to sell, I know he won't ask for any part of the proceeds regardless of his legal right to those funds."

And all that may be true, but it may cost you more in taxes to sell your property than if you kept the property in your name only.

Under today's law, you can sell your home without paying a Capital Gains Tax, provided you lived there for 2 of the prior 5 years and the Capital Gains on the sale is not greater than $250,000 ($500,000 if married). If you sell your home after making the Life Estate transfer (or making your child a Joint Tenant), then unless your child occupies the home as his primary residence, his share of the property is subject to a Capital Gains Tax.

If your son does not take his share of the proceeds, then why should he pay any Capital Gains Tax?

In such case, you'll be the one to pay the tax on your son's share of the proceeds.

Is there a better way to avoid Probate?

Maybe. Read on.

How To Avoid Probate   3

TRUE OR FALSE?

( ) If you have a Will, then Probate will be necessary.

( ) Probate will be necessary if you don't have a Will.

( ) A Formal Probate is necessary if you own property worth more than $75,000.

If you answered false to all of the above, you are either a lawyer, or you carefully read the last chapter.

All of these sentences are false because all of your property may pass to your beneficiaries automatically, without the need for Probate, such as property held jointly or in a Pay On Death account. The point we were trying to make is:

> Whether Probate is necessary has nothing to do with whether there is a Will, or even how much money is involved. The determining factor is how the property is titled (owned).

There are three basic ways to title property:

◇ in your name only

◇ jointly with another

◇ in trust for another

Chapter 1 examined the pros and cons of holding property in your name only, with the biggest "con" being that Probate may be necessary.

In Chapter 2 we noted that holding property jointly with another solved the Probate problem, but at the sacrifice of the control and protection offered by keeping property in your name only. In this Chapter we examine another option which may be the solution to these problems, namely the **Revocable Living Trust**, which is also known as an *Inter Vivos Trust* (FS 689.075).

A Revocable Living Trust is designed to care for your property during your lifetime and then to distribute your property once you die without the need for Probate. You may have been encouraged to set up such a Trust by your financial planner, attorney, or accountant. Even people of modest means are being encouraged to use a Trust as the basis of their Estate Plan. But Trusts also have their pros and cons.

Before getting into that, let's first discuss what a Trust is and how it works.

HOW A TRUST IS CREATED

To create a **Revocable Living Trust,** an attorney prepares a Trust Agreement in accordance with the client's needs and desires. The "Agreement" refers to the fact that the person setting up the Trust (the *Trustor* or *Settlor)* is contracting with someone to be the **Trustee** (manager) property placed in the Trust. By signing the Trust Agreement, the Trustee agrees to manage the Trust property according to the directions given in the Trust Agreement. If the Trustor is the one who places property into the Trust, then he is referred to as the **Grantor.** The Trust Agreement also names a **Successor Trustee** who will take over the management of the Trust property should the Grantor resign, become disabled or die.

We will refer to the Revocable Living Trust as the "Living Trust" or just the "Trust" and the person setting up the Trust as the "Grantor." Usually the Grantor appoints himself as the initial Trustee so that he is in total control of property that he places into the Trust. In that case he signs the Trust Agreement as the Grantor and also as the Trustee who agrees to follow the terms of the Trust Agreement.

Once the Trust document is properly signed, the Grantor can transfer property into the Trust. The Grantor does this by changing the name on the account from his individual name to his name as Trustee. For example, if Elaine Richards sets up a Trust naming herself as Trustee, and she wants to put her bank account into the Trust, all she needs to do is instruct the bank to change the name on the account from Elaine Richards to:

ELAINE RICHARDS, TRUSTEE OF THE ELAINE RICHARDS
REVOCABLE LIVING TRUST
UNDER AGREEMENT DATED JULY 12, 2004.

If Elaine wants to put real property that she owns into the Trust, she can have her attorney or a title insurance company prepare and record a new deed with the owner of the property identified as:

ELAINE RICHARDS, TRUSTEE OF THE ELAINE RICHARDS
REVOCABLE TRUST AGREEMENT
UNDER AGREEMENT DATED JULY 12, 2004.

The Trust Agreement states how property placed into the Trust is to be managed during Elaine's lifetime. Generally it provides for the Trustee to have total control of the Trust property. For example, monies held in a Trust bank account can be withdrawn or added to in the same manner as if Elaine held the property in her name only. Because the Trust is revocable, Elaine can cancel the Trust at any time and have the Trust property put back into her own name.

If Elaine does not revoke the Trust during her lifetime, once she dies the Trust becomes irrevocable. Her Successor Trustee is required to follow the terms of the Trust Agreement as it is written. If the Trust says to give the Trust property to certain beneficiaries, the Successor Trustee will do so; and in most cases without any Probate procedure. If the Trust directs the Successor Trustee to continue to hold property in Trust and use the money to take care of a member of Elaine's family, then it is the job of the Successor Trustee to use the money to care for the family member in the manner described in the Trust Agreement.

The Successor Trustee must also follow Florida statutes relating to the administration of the Trust. For example, within 30 days, the Successor Trustee must inform all of the beneficiaries, in writing, that he is now administering the Trust, and upon request, must provide the beneficiary with a copy of the Trust (FS 737.303).

THE PROS AND CONS OF A TRUST

A Living Trust has many good features.

☆ AVOID PROBATE

As discussed in Chapter 1, Probate can be time consuming and expensive. Both the Personal Representative and his attorney are entitled to payment for their services. These fees can be significant. It may be necessary to hire accountants and appraisers, as well. If you have property in two states, then two Probate procedures may be necessary (one in each state) and that could have the effect of doubling the cost of Probate. If the Trust is properly drafted and your property placed into the Trust, you should be able to avoid Probate altogether.

☆ PRIVACY

Your Trust is a private document. No one but your Successor Trustee and your beneficiaries need ever read it. When opening a bank account in the name of the Trust, the bank might ask for a copy of the Trust Agreement, but all they need is basic information about the Trust such as the date of execution of the Trust; the Trust tax identification number; the identity of the Grantor, the current Trustee, the identity of Successor Trustee and the beneficiaries of the Trust, etc. You attorney can prepare a *Certificate of Trust* to give to the bank that contains this basic information.

If you have a Will, once it is admitted to Probate it becomes part of the Court records. Anyone can examine the Court records, read your Will and see who you did (or did not) provide for. Other Probate documents such as the inventory of your Probate Estate, creditor's claims, etc. are also open to public scrutiny. In Florida, Court records are now available on the Internet!

LEASE SAFE DEPOSIT BOX AS TRUSTEE

Another privacy issue is what happens to the contents your safe deposit box, should you become disabled or die. Under Florida law, if you hold a safe deposit box in your name only, then once the bank (or other safe deposit box lessor) learns of your death, access to the box is restricted. The bank may allow your spouse, parent, child, or the person you named as the Executor of your Will, to look at the contents of the box under the supervision of an officer or employee of the company. The bank will allow any of these people to take possession of the Will or a deed to a burial plot, or life insurance policy. Nothing else can be removed from the safe deposit box without authority from the Probate Court (FS 655.935).

By leasing the safe deposit box in your capacity as Trustee, you can avoid having the bank officer (or anyone other than your Successor Trustee) examine the contents of your safe deposit box. You can instruct the bank that upon your death or disability, your Successor Trustee has full authority to enter the box and remove any and all of the items from that box.

☆ CARE FOR FAMILY MEMBER

You can make provision in your Trust to care for a minor child or family member after you die. If your family member is immature or a born spender, you can set up the Trust to protect the beneficiary from squandering the inheritance. If you are concerned that your beneficiary will spend, within months, what it took you a lifetime to earn, consider having an attorney prepare a Trust that will spread the inheritance over an extended period of time. Your Trust can direct the Trustee to give a certain amount of money every 5 or 10 years; for example you can direct the Trustee to give part of the gift when the beneficiary reaches 25, another amount when he reaches 35, and then 45, etc.

If your intended beneficiary has a creditor problem, you can set up a *Spendthrift Trust*. You can direct your Successor Trustee to use the Trust funds for your beneficiary's health care, education, and living expenses, and nothing else. With a properly drafted Spendthrift Trust provision the Trust funds should be protected from the claims of the creditors of the beneficiary.

NO CREDITOR PROTECTION FOR GRANTOR

Although you can set up a Spendthrift Trust for the benefit of a family member, you cannot set one up for yourself. Property you place in your Revocable Living Trust is freely accessible to you. It is likewise accessible to your creditors both before and after your death. If you die owing money, your creditors can have a Personal Representative appointed to locate funds to pay those debts. The Personal Representative can require that your Trust property be used to pay for those debts as well as for other expenses associated with the Probate procedure (FS 733.707, 737.3054).

NO CREDITOR PROTECTION FOR THE HOME

Because there is no creditor protection for items placed in the Trust, it is prudent not to place your homestead into your Trust. There is creditor protection for property you own and occupy in Florida as your primary residence; but a recent bankruptcy court denied creditor protection to homestead property that the owner held as Trustee of her Revocable Trust Agreement (*Crews v. Bosonetto (In re Bosonetto)*, 271 B.R. 403 (Bankr. M.D. Fla. 2001). If you are married, it is better to own your homestead together with your spouse as Tenants by the Entirety. If you are single you may want to keep your homestead in your name only even if it means that a Probate procedure will be necessary to transfer the property to your beneficiary.

☆ AVOID A CHALLENGE TO YOUR ESTATE PLAN

A Trust operates much like a Will because it provides for the distribution of your Estate when you die. Unlike a Will, it is not subject to Probate, so no Court is charged with the duty of "proving" that your Trust is valid. Your Successor Trustee can distribute your property as you direct, without asking anyone's permission to do so; understanding however, that Trust funds may be needed to pay outstanding debts.

Florida law requires that upon the death of the Grantor of an Inter Vivos Trust, the Trustee must file a Notice of Trust in the Probate Court of the Grantor's residence, giving the Grantor's date of death, and the name and address of the Trustee. By giving such notice, the Grantor's creditors are made aware of the Trust and they can require payment from the Trustee in the manner just described (FS 737.308, 733.607).

☆☆ AVOID GUARDIANSHIP

Once you have a Trust, you do not need to worry about who will take care of your property should you become disabled or too aged to handle your finances. The person you appointed as Successor Trustee will take over the care of the Trust property if you are unable to do so. If you do not have a Trust, and become incapacitated, a Court may need to appoint a Guardian to care for your property. The cost to establish and maintain the guardianship is charged to you. As we will see in Chapter 9, such legal procedures can be expensive; and once established cannot be terminated unless you die or are restored to health (FS 744.521).

With all these perks, you may be ready to call your attorney to make an appointment to set up a Trust, but before doing so there are a few things you need to consider.

THE CONS

☒ COMPLEXITY

A Trust is a fairly complex document, often more than 20 pages long. It needs to be that long because you are establishing a vehicle for taking care of your property during your lifetime, as well as after your death. Your Trust may be written in "legalese," so it may take you considerable time and effort to understand it. It is important to have your Trust document prepared by an attorney who has the patience to work with you until you fully understand each paragraph of the document and are satisfied that what it states is what you really want.

It is also important that you read Florida statute 737.402. That statute gives your Successor Trustee the power to do all of the things as allowed by that statute, unless your Trust specifically prohibits your Successor Trustee from doing so. For example, under 737.402, your Trustee has the power to terminate the Trust whenever the market value of the Trust property is $50,000 or less. If you have included a Spendthrift Trust, you may not want your Successor Trustee to just hand $50,000 to your beneficiary. In such case, it is important that your Trust Agreement state that 737.402 shall not apply to the termination of the Spendthrift Trust.

☒ COST

Because of the thoroughness of the document and the fact that it is custom designed for you, a Trust will cost much more to draft than a simple Will. In addition to the initial cost of the Trust, it can be expensive to maintain the Trust should you become disabled or die. Your Successor Trustee has the right to charge for his duties as Trustee, as well as to charge for any specialized services performed.

A financial institution can charge to serve as Successor Trustee, and also charge to manage the Trust portfolio. If you decide to have a financial institution serve as Trustee, then it is important that you compare the fee schedules of different institutions.

If you choose a professional (lawyer, accountant, financial planner, etc.) to serve as Trustee, it is important to have a fee agreement stating what will be charged for his duties as Trustee and what will be charged for professional work done on behalf of the Trust. If you make no provision, the professional is entitled to the going rate for work done in relation to a Trust. And that fee can be substantial. Under Florida law, a reasonable fee for a Trustee's attorney is 75% of the schedule charged by the attorney of a Probate Estate (see page 22) (FS 737.2041).

Still another concern with choosing a professional to serve as Trustee is that it creates a conflict of interest. The professional can use his position as Trustee to generate fees for himself or his firm.

You may decide to appoint your spouse or a family member as Successor Trustee, who may want little, or no, compensation. Regardless of who you choose to be Successor Trustee, you need to come to an agreement as to what will be charged to manage the Trust. If you make no provision for fees in your Trust Agreement, your Successor Trustee has the right to take a reasonable fee from the Trust property. If the beneficiaries of the Trust do not think the fee reasonable, they can ask to the Court to set the fee (FS 737.204).

But that will probably trigger a legal battle. It is better that you set the fee. Hopefully, that will head off unnecessary legal fees.

☒ YOU MAY NEED YOUR SPOUSE'S PERMISSION
     TO TRANSFER PROPERTY INTO YOUR TRUST

Most married couples prepare a Trust as part of their overall Estate Plan. Sometimes a married person has a Trust that was prepared prior to the marriage, or he may decide to create a Trust to care for children from a previous marriage. In such case, it may be necessary to have the spouse agree, in writing, to transfers into the Trust. The reason permission is needed is the **Elective Share**. The Grantor's spouse has a right to inherit at least as much as allowed under Florida law, unless the spouse signs a waiver giving up that right. In Florida, the Elective Share is equal to 30% of the **Elective Estate** of the decedent spouse (FS 732.201, 732.2065).

The Elective Estate includes:
⇨ Property held in the decedent's Living Trust
⇨ The decedent's Probate Estate
⇨ Any gift in excess of $10,000 given by the decedent within 1 year of his death
⇨ The decedent's ownership interest in joint bank accounts, In Trust For or Pay On Death accounts, Transfer On Death securities, etc. (FS 732.2045).

The proceeds of a life insurance policy are not included in the Elective Estate, however, the cash surrender value of the policy immediately before the date of death is included. See FS 732.2035 for a complete list of property included in the Elective Estate.

If you make transfers into your Trust without your spouse's permission, and without providing that your spouse receive 30% of your Elective Estate, your spouse can go to the Probate Court and demand that as much property be transferred from the Trust (or from anyone in possession of your property) as is necessary to make up the Elective Share (FS 732.2145).

⊠ PROBATE MIGHT STILL BE NECESSARY

The Trust only works for those items that you place in the Trust. Property owned in your name only will require some type of Probate procedure to transfer it to your beneficiary. For example, if you buy a security in your name only, without a Transfer On Death designation to your Trust or to a named beneficiary, then a Probate proceeding will be necessary to transfer that security to your beneficiary. The decision not to place all of your property into your Trust might be intentional. As explained on page 47, keeping your homestead in your name gives you maximum creditor protection, so you may not want it to go into your Trust during your lifetime.

Your attorney will prepare a Will for you to sign at the same time you sign the Trust. The Will prepared by the attorney is called a *Pour Over Will* because it is designed to "pour" any asset titled in your name only, into the Trust. The Will directs your Personal Representative to transfer your Probate assets to your Successor Trustee to be placed into your Trust, and then distributed to the beneficiaries named in your Trust (FS 732.513).

You can ensure that a Probate procedure will not be necessary by transferring your assets into your Trust during your lifetime, or holding them jointly or in beneficiary form, but if you have your homestead or any other asset in your name only, the Pour Over Will stands by to transfer that asset into your Trust.

⊠ FLORIDA TRUSTS DRAFTED AFTER 1/1/01 CAN BE CHANGED BY THE TRUSTEE AND BENEFICIARIES

In the year 2000, the Florida legislature passed a law (FS 737.4032) that effectively gives the Successor Trustee and the beneficiaries of the Trust, the power to do whatever they wish with Trust property once the Grantor dies. Specifically, for Trusts created after January 1, 2001, regardless of what the Trust says, the Trustee, with the unanimous agreement of all of the beneficiaries, can do any of the following:

⇨ change any of the terms on the Trust, including changing the beneficiaries of the Trust and/or the income or principal each beneficiary is to receive

⇨ terminate the Trust altogether

⇨ stop the Trustee from doing things required by the Trust Agreement

⇨ allow the Trustee to do things strictly prohibited by the Trust Agreement.

Before this law was passed, once the Grantor of an Inter Vivos Trust died, the Trust became irrevocable and could not be changed without permission by a Court. With this law, the Trustee, together with the beneficiaries, can alter the terms of the Trust without asking for the permission of the Court, or anyone else, to do so.

If it is important to you as Grantor, that your Trust Agreement be honored, you need to choose a Trustee who will follow the provisions of the Trust, regardless of requests or demands made by the beneficiaries.

⊠ ☆ THE TRUST IS LEGALLY ENFORCEABLE

Any beneficiary, or Trustee, of the Trust can ask the Court to settle a dispute arising out of the administration of the Trust. Florida law requires that the Trustee keep the beneficiaries reasonably informed of the Trust assets and how the Trust is being administered. The Trustee must give the beneficiaries an annual accounting. If the Trustee is abusing his power or not accounting for Trust funds, the beneficiaries can ask the Court to have the Trustee removed (FS 737.201, 737.303).

We gave this section a cross and a star, because the right to have a Trust enforced or administered by a Court is a double edged sword. It is great to have the Court protect the rights of your beneficiaries, but the cost of a Court battle could be greater than using Probate to transfer your Estate. Worse yet, your beneficiaries are at a disadvantage because the Trustee can charge the legal expenses to your Trust, while the beneficiaries must pay for their legal battles out of their own pocket. Even if the beneficiaries win the argument, the Trustee's legal fees are paid from the Trust, so there is just that much less for the beneficiaries to inherit.

TAXES AND YOUR TRUST

Putting property into a Revocable Living Trust does not shield that property from taxes. All of the property held in a Revocable Living Trust is taxed as if the Grantor were holding that property in his own name. If the property earns income, then income taxes will be due, and at the same rate as the Grantor would have paid if he had no Trust. Once the Grantor dies, both the federal and state government have the right to impose an *Estate Tax* on property transferred to a beneficiary as a result of the death. All the property owned as of the date of death becomes the decedent's *Taxable Estate.* This includes *real property* (residential lots, condominiums, etc.) and *personal property* (cars, life insurance policies, business interests, securities, IRA accounts, etc.). It includes property held in the decedent's name alone, as well as property that he held jointly or in Trust. It also includes gifts given by the decedent during his lifetime that exceeded $10,000 per person, per year. In the year 2002, the *Annual Gift Tax Exclusion* of $10,000 was increased to $11,000 to adjust for inflation (IRC 2503(b)).

For most of us, this is not a concern because no federal or Florida Estate Tax need be paid unless the decedent's Taxable Estate exceeds the federal *Estate Tax Exclusion* amount. That value is currently one and a half million dollars and is scheduled to go even higher.

YEAR	ESTATE TAX EXCLUSION AMOUNT
2004-2005	$1,500,000
2006-2008	$2,000,000
2009	$3,500,000

In 2010 the federal Estate Tax is scheduled to be phased out altogether; however in 2011, the Estate Tax will be reinstated with an Exclusion Amount of $1,000,000 unless lawmakers change the tax law once again.

The Florida Estate tax is based on the federal Estate Tax. The federal government imposes a tax on all property transferred because of the death. The federal government then grants an Estate Tax credit, so that no tax need be paid unless the amount transferred is more than a given dollar value. We have referred to that dollar value as the federal Estate Tax Exclusion amount (currently one million dollars). The Florida Estate tax is called a "pick-up" tax, because the state collects the tax that would have gone to the federal government had it not been for the federal Estate Tax credit.

As with the federal Estate Tax, no tax need be paid to the state of Florida, unless the decedent's Taxable Estate exceeds the current federal Tax Exclusion amount. But for those Estate that are larger than the Exclusion value, Estate taxes will need to be paid to the federal government and to the state of Florida. And that includes property transferred within the state of Florida regardless of whether the decedent was a resident of the state (FS 198.01, 198.02, 198.03).

As explained, the federal Estate Tax is scheduled to be phased out and then reinstated in 2011. The Florida Estate Tax is based on the federal Estate Tax credit, so unless the Florida legislature changes things, the Florida Estate Tax will go the way of the federal Estate Tax.

Both state and federal government do not tax property passing to the decedent's spouse, however, once the surviving spouse dies, all of his/her Estate is subject to Estate taxes. As explained on the next page, setting up a Revocable Living Trust can significantly reduce the amount of federal and Florida Estate taxes that may need to be paid once the surviving spouse dies.

A TRUST TO REDUCE ESTATE TAXES

Under current law, Estates of those who die in 2010 are exempt from Federal Estate taxes, but in 2011, the Estate Tax is scheduled to be reinstated and Estates worth more than $1,000,000 will once again be subject to a sizeable Estate Tax. A couple with an Estate in excess of a million dollars can reduce the risk of an Estate Tax by setting up his and her Trusts, so that each person can take advantage of his own Exclusion Amount.

For example, if a husband and wife own 2 million dollars, they can separate their funds into two Trusts each valued at one million dollars. The Trusts can be set up so that a surviving spouse can use the income from the deceased partner's Trust for living expenses. In this way, their standard of living need not be reduced by separating their funds into two Trusts.

If they do not wish to separate funds, they can set up a single Joint Trust that separates into two Trusts once one partner dies. Again, the surviving spouse is free to use the income from both Trusts. Once both partners are deceased, the beneficiaries of their respective Trusts will inherit the funds, hopefully with no Estate Tax due.

If the couple makes no Trust provision, and they hold their property jointly, the last to die will own the two million dollars with only one Estate Tax Exclusion available. If lawmakers do not change the tax law, and the surviving spouse dies in 2011, or later, one million dollars of their Estate will be subject to an Estate Tax.

A Revocable Living Trust is a relatively simple way for a married couple to reduce, if not eliminate, the need to pay Estate taxes; however, there is still the problem of the federal Gift Tax and the Capital Gains Tax.

THE UN-UNIFIED GIFT TAX

Up until the year 2002, if you gave someone more than $10,000 in any given year you had to report that gift to the IRS. As explained, the Annual Gift Tax Exclusion is now adjusted for the cost of living and is currently $11,000. The IRS keeps a running count of amounts that you give over the Annual Gift Tax Exclusion. Although you are required to report the gift, no tax need be paid unless that running total is more than the federal Estate Tax Exclusion amount. If your running total does not exceed that amount during your lifetime, once you die, the cumulative value of gifts reported to the IRS will be added to your Taxable Estate.

Until the tax law was changed, the Gift and Estate tax were unified. No Gift Tax needed to be paid unless the total value of the taxable gifts exceeded the federal Estate Tax Exclusion amount. In 2004 that changed. The Estate Tax Exclusion amount went up to $1,500,000, but the amount for the Gift Tax Exclusion remained at $1,000,000, so they now are no longer unified.

To summarize:
If you make a gift to anyone that is greater than the Annual Gift Tax Exclusion for that year, you must report the gift to the IRS. The IRS will keep count of values that you gave in excess of the Annual Gift Tax Exclusion. In 2004, and thereafter, if that sum exceeds $1,000,000, you will pay a Gift Tax on any amount you give that is over the Annual Gift Tax Exclusion.

The Estate Tax is scheduled to be repealed in 2010, but not the Gift Tax.

The current federal Estate Tax is scheduled to be phased out in the year 2010, but a new Capital Gains Tax is scheduled for 2010 that may prove even more costly than the Estate Tax. The new Capital Gains Tax is related to the way inherited property is evaluated by the federal government. Real and personal property is inherited at a "step-up" in basis, meaning that if the decedent's property has increased in value from the time he acquired it, the beneficiary will inherit the property at its fair market value as of the decedent's date of death. For example, if the decedent bought stock for $20,000 and it is worth $50,000 as of his date of death, the beneficiary will take a step-up in basis of $30,000; i.e. the beneficiary inherits the stock at the current $50,000 value. If the beneficiary sells the stock for $50,000, he pays no Capital Gains Tax. If the beneficiary holds onto the stock and later sells it for $60,000, the beneficiary will pay a Capital Gains Tax only on the $10,000 increase in value since the decedent's death.

Up to 2009, there is no limit to the amount a beneficiary can take as a step-up in basis. But in 2010 caps are set in place. The decedent's Estate will be allowed a 1.3 million dollar step-up in basis, plus another 3 million for property passing to the surviving spouse (IRS Code 1022(b)). The new law could result in significant Capital Gains Taxes that the beneficiary must pay. For example, suppose in 2010 you inherit a business from your father that he purchased for $100,000 and it is now worth 2 million dollars. There is a capital gain of 1.9 million dollars, but you are allowed a step-up in basis of only 1.3 million. If you sell it for 2 million dollars $600,000 of your inheritance will be subject to a Capital Gains Tax.

We will discuss methods of reducing the Gift Tax and the Capital Gains Tax in Chapter 7.

Although many methods can be used to transfer property without the need for Probate, it may be that each of them has a downside that is objectionable to you. Maybe you don't have enough money to warrant the cost of setting up the Trust at this time. Holding property jointly with another may raise issues of security and independence. Holding property so that it goes directly to a few beneficiaries in a Pay On Death account may not be as flexible as you wish. This may be the case if you want to give gifts to several charities or to a minor children.

For example, you can hold all your property so that it goes directly to your son without the need for Probate. If you ask him to use some of the money for your grandchild's education, it may be that your grandchild gets none of the money because your son is sued or falls upon hard times. If you keep your property in your name only and leave a Will giving a certain amount of money to your grandchild, the child will know exactly how much money you left and the purpose of that gift.

After taking into account all the pros and cons of avoiding Probate, you may decide to opt for a Will and a Probate procedure. If you make such a decision, it is important to keep in mind that Estate Planning is not an "all or nothing" choice. You can arrange your Estate so that certain items pass automatically to your intended beneficiary, and other items can be left in your name only, to be distributed as part of a Probate procedure. By arranging your finances in this manner, you can reduce the value of your Probate Estate, and that in turn should reduce the cost of Probate.

In the next chapter, we discuss the Will as an Estate Planning tool.

Those of you who have a Will may be thinking that there is no reason to read the Chapter, but does your Will:

▤   Make provision for the amount to be paid to your Personal Representative?

▤   Make gifts of your personal property? (jewelry, car, etc.)

▤   Name a Guardian to care for your minor child?

▤   Make adjustment for gifts or loans that you gave to the beneficiaries of your Will?

▤   Give specific instructions about how your bills and taxes are to be paid; i.e., which of your beneficiaries will have his inheritance reduced in order to pay your debts and taxes?

Has your Will been prepared so that it will be difficult for anyone to challenge it?

Have you stored your Will so that it is safe AND easily accessible to you during your lifetime and to your Personal Representative after your death?

If you answered "Yes" to all of the above questions, then you can skip over to Chapter 5.

Your Will – Your Way   4

Many people decide that the Will is the best route to go but do not act upon it, thinking it unnecessary to prepare a Will until they are very old and about to die. But according to reports published by the National Center for Health Statistics (a division of the U.S. Department of Health and Human Services) 2 of every 10 people who die in any given year are under the age of 60. Twenty percent may seem like a small number until it hits close to home as it did with a young couple.

Alex and Cathy were an old-fashioned couple in a modern world. When they married, they knew they wanted a large family. There was no question that Cathy would stay home and raise the children while Alex went to work. Luckily he did very well as one of the managers of a string of restaurants. Better yet, he enjoyed his work. He loved to cook and would even take over the kitchen when he returned from work. That suited Cathy just fine because she had her hands full raising their three boys.

Cathy couldn't help thinking how lucky they were that morning as she fixed breakfast. A nice house. Healthy, if not rambunctious, boys. All in all, a comfortable marriage. Her only concern that day was the fact that Alex was flying off on a business trip. All this terrorist news made her nervous about flying. Alex reassured her that it was only an hour's flight, and besides he was flying the company plane and not a commercial airliner.

But it was not terrorists that brought down the plane, just a malfunctioning rudder.

THINGS A WILL CAN DO

Though we all agree that one never knows, still people put off making a Will, figuring that if they die before getting around to it, Florida law will take over and their property will be distributed in the manner that they would have wanted anyway. The problem with that logic is the complexity of Florida's Laws of Intestate Succession. It isn't too difficult to figure out who will inherit your property, if you are survived by a spouse, child, parent or sibling. But if none of these survive you, the ultimate beneficiary of your property may not be the person you would have chosen, had you taken the time to do so.

Others think that it is not necessary to have a Will because they have arranged their finances so that all of their property will be inherited without the need for Probate. But money could come into your Estate after your death. This could happen in any number of ways from winning the lottery and dying (of happiness, no doubt) to receiving insurance funds after your death. For example, if you die in a house fire, the company that insures your home may need to pay for damages done to the property. In such case, the funds will need to be paid to your Estate. A Personal Representative may need to be appointed and the insurance funds distributed according to Florida law.

If you die without a Will, your Estate may be distributed differently than you would have wished. And there are other important reasons to make a Will.

APPOINT PERSONAL REPRESENTATIVE

The Court will give top priority to the person you name as Personal Representative of your Will. Without a Will, the Court will use the following order of priority to decide who will serve as your Personal Representative.

1st   the surviving spouse

2nd   the person selected by those entitled to inherit a majority of the Estate

3rd   the nearest next of kin as determined by the Laws of Intestate Succession.

If two or more with the same priority want the job and cannot come to an agreement, then the Court will decide who should serve (FS 733.301).

ARRANGE FOR PERSONAL REPRESENTATIVE FEES

Once you decide on a Personal Representative, you need check with that person to be sure that he is willing to serve in that capacity. And if so, then you should come to an understanding about how much compensation he will receive to settle your Estate. If you do not make provision for his fee, then he is entitled to receive the amount as stated under Florida law (FS 733.617).

That fee is substantial. For example, an Estate worth $100,000 will pay $3,000 in fees to the Personal Representative (see Chapter 1).

Once you and your Personal Representative agree upon a rate of compensation, you can have your attorney include the fee agreement in your Will.

THE PERSONAL REPRESENTATIVE CAN SEEK MORE MONEY

You can put the amount of compensation to be paid to your Personal Representative in your Will; however, under Florida law he can reject that amount and ask for the amount allowed under Florida statute 733.617. To avoid the problem, you can have your attorney draft an Agreement that you and your Personal Representative sign and attach it to your Will. Having a separate fee Agreement will not stop your Personal Representative from asking for more money, but with such an Agreement, the Court will not agree to the increase unless something unusual occurs (such as a law suit) causing much more work than the ordinary Probate procedure.

You also need to keep in mind that the Personal Representative's fee is just to administer the Estate. It does not include payment for professional work he may do while settling the Estate. For example, if you appoint your attorney as Personal Representative, he can agree to the amount stated in the Will for his role as Personal Representative, and then ask the Court to award him attorney's fees as well.

The same goes for any other professional. If you appoint your accountant to serve as Personal Representative, he is entitled to receive compensation for his work as Personal Representative and also for any accounting work he does such as preparing and filing tax returns, preparing an inventory and doing an accounting for the beneficiaries. A financial planner who serves as Personal Representative may be compensated for his management of the Estate property (buying and selling securities, taking care of rental property, etc.) in addition to his fee to administer the Estate.

But the main problem with appointing a professional as your Personal Representative is the same as appointing a professional to serve as the Successor Trustee of your Trust; namely, that it creates a potential conflict of interest. The professional could use his position as Personal Representative to generate fees that might not have been necessary had someone else settled the Estate.

Unless the professional is the sole beneficiary of your Will, it is better to chose a non-professional to settle your Estate.

▤ MAKE GIFTS OF YOUR PERSONAL PROPERTY

Another benefit to making a Will is that you can make provision for who will get your *personal property* (securities, boats, snowmobiles etc.). When making a Will consider making provision for your car. If you make a *specific gift* i.e. a gift to a named beneficiary of your Will, it will be relatively simple for your Personal Representative to transfer the car to your beneficiary. If you do not make a specific gift of your car, then your Personal Representative will decide what to do with it. He may decide to sell it and include the proceeds of the sale in the Estate funds to be distributed as part of the Probate Estate; or he can give the car to one beneficiary of your Estate as part of that beneficiary's share of the Estate.

SMALL GIFTS MATTER

Many who have lost someone close to them report that the distribution of small personal items caused the greatest conflict. If you arrange your finances so that no Probate procedure is necessary, your next of kin will need to decide among themselves how to distribute your personal effects. Without guidance from you and no Personal Representative with authority to make decisions, there could be disagreement and hard feelings over items of little monetary value, but much sentimental value.

You can make gifts of your *personal effects* (clothing, books, music collection, etc.) by making a list of these gifts, clearly identifying the gift and the person who is to receive the gift. Your Personal Representative will distribute your personal effects according to that list. You can change the list at any time just so long as you sign and date the list. No witness to your signature is needed. The list is for items with more sentimental than monetary value. You should not include money gifts, expensive jewelry, items used in your business, or real property in the list. Those items need to be given as part of your Will (FS 732.15).

Of course it is impossible to make a list of every single item you own. You can leave instructions in your Will to have certain family members take their choice of items not mentioned in your Will. If two or more family members want the same item, have your Personal Representative use an appropriate lottery system (toss of coin, high card in a cut of a deck of cards, etc.) to decide who "wins."

 YOU CAN'T GIVE WHAT YOU DON'T HAVE

You need to give considerable thought whenever you make a specific gift to someone. It could be that you no longer own the item at the time of your death. This could happen with property or money. For example, suppose you leave all of your Estate to your son, with a specific gift of $10,000 to each of your three grandchildren. Your son is the *residuary beneficiary* of the Probate Estate, meaning he gets whatever is left once all of the bills are paid and all of the specific gifts made. If the cost of your last illness leaves your Probate Estate with only $30,000 to distribute, would you want the grandchildren to get their gifts and your son nothing?

The simple solution is to make all of them residuary beneficiaries by leaving each a percent of your Estate. For example, instead of making a specific gift to each grandchild you could leave 70% to your son and 10% to each grandchild.

NON-PROBATE ASSETS

Property held in a Pay On Death account, the proceeds of a life insurance policy, Trust property and IRA accounts are all *Non-probate* assets because they will be inherited by your named beneficiary without the need for Probate. You cannot make a gift of such property in your Will because, you have, in effect, already made a gift of these assets. The beneficiary of a Non-probate asset can only be changed by the owner of the property during his lifetime. The beneficiary of a Non-probate asset cannot be changed by Will (FS 711.509). Unless you named your Estate as the beneficiary of a Non-probate asset, it should not be mentioned in your Will. To do so might cause your Will to be challenged by whoever was named as the beneficiary of the Non-probate asset.

THE SPOUSE'S RIGHT TO A LIFE ESTATE

If your Florida home is in your name only, and it is your primary residence, then under Florida law, your surviving spouse has the right to continue to live in your home for the rest of his/her life. Once your spouse is deceased, your children inherit the home in equal shares, per stirpes. You can make a Will giving the house to your spouse, but only if you do not have minor children. If you have minor children, regardless of what your Will says, your spouse has a Life Estate with remainder to your children (FS 732. 401, 732.4015). If you want your spouse to inherit your home, minor children or not, have your attorney change the deed so that your home is owned by you and your spouse as Tenants by the Entirety.

MINOR CHILD'S RIGHT TO THE HOMESTEAD

Married or single, if you have minor children, they have rights in your homestead. Specifically, under the Florida Constitution, if you own your home in your name only and are single with minor children, with or without a Will, your children inherit your homestead, in equal shares, per stirpes (Florida Constitution Article X, Section 4(c)).

Of course, if you are single, without minor children, you are free to give that property to any beneficiary you name in your Will.

CHOOSE A GUARDIAN FOR YOUR MINOR CHILD

If one parent dies, then it is the right, and duty, of the surviving parent to care for the child (FS 744.301). But it could happen that both parents become incapacitated or die before the child is grown. If you have a minor child, you can use your Will to appoint someone to serve as the Guardian of your minor child in the event that both you and the other parent are deceased (FS 744.312). You can even include a Trust in your Will, naming someone to serve as Trustee to care for property that you leave to your minor child.

See Chapter 7 for more information about how to make provision for the care of your minor child in the event of your incapacity, or death.

You can make adjustments in your Will for gifts or loans given during your lifetime. For example, if you have loaned money to a family member and do not expect to be repaid, you can deduct the loan from that person's inheritance. There is no need to make the adjustment if the borrower gives you a promissory note because should you die, the monies will be owed to your Estate and the Personal Representative can deduct the monies owed from the borrower's inheritance. But if there is no evidence of the debt and you neglect to make a Will, the borrower will receive his full share as provided under Florida's Laws of Intestate Succession (FS 732.609).

That was the case with Sally and Tom. They were firm believers in treating each of their four children equally. "Share and share alike" was their favorite saying. Once Tom died, Sally continued with the tradition, never giving to one child, without giving something of equal value, to each of the other three

Sally did not think of the loan she gave to her son as a gift. After all, he promised to pay it back, with interest. She did not ask her son to sign a promissory note. He was family. If you can't trust your own son, who can you trust?

The son was prompt with his monthly payments. But only two payments were made before his mother died suddenly, from a heart attack.

Sally never mentioned the loan to any of her other children. Neither did her son. Each child received one fourth of their mother's Estate; and none the wiser. Except whenever Sally's son dreams of his mother, she is not smiling.

MAKE PROVISION FOR PAYMENT OF DEBTS

Most Wills contain an instruction to the Personal Representative to ". . . pay all the expenses of my last illness, funeral expenses, costs of administration, taxes and just debts. . . " Under Florida law, paying all of your debts does not include paying off a loan on a gift made to a beneficiary.

For example, if you leave your car to a beneficiary, and you have a loan on the car, you need to specify whether you want the loan to be paid from your Probate Estate so that your beneficiary will inherit the car free and clear, or whether you want to have your beneficiary be responsible to pay off the loan. If you make no provision in your Will, then under Florida law, your beneficiary will inherit the loan along with the car (FS 733.803).

This same rule applies even if you do not make a specific gift of the item. For example, if there is a mortgage on your home, and you make no mention of who is to inherit the home, then it will be inherited by your residuary beneficiaries; and they will be responsible to pay off the loan.

They can use the Estate funds to do so, but if there is not enough money in the Estate to pay off the loan, whoever takes title to the property will need to pay the debt or make arrangements to refinance the property.

MAKE PROVISION FOR PAYMENT OF TAXES

Taxes are another concern for those Estates large enough to be subject to Estate Taxes. If you make no provision in your Will or Trust for the payment of Estate Taxes, then the person who is ultimately responsible to pay those taxes is determined by state and federal law.

NON-PROBATE ASSETS

The beneficiary of certain Non-probate assets such as the beneficiary of a Pay-On-Death account, the beneficiary of a life insurance policy, the surviving joint owner of real property, etc., must pay his share of Estate Taxes. If a beneficiary refuses to contribute his share of the taxes, whoever is required to make payment (usually the Personal Representative or the surviving spouse) can ask the Court to order the beneficiary to contribute his share of the taxes (26 U.S.C. 6324 (a)(2), FS 733.817).

PROBATE TRANSFERS

Estate Taxes due on Probate transfers are paid from the *Residuary Estate* i.e., whatever is left once all specific gifts have been made. This means that the beneficiary of a specific gift is not responsible to pay Estate Taxes on that gift, unless there is not enough money in the Residuary Estate to pay those taxes; and in that case the beneficiary of the gift must contribute his share of the taxes.

INTER VIVOS TRUST TRANSFERS

Estate Taxes due on transfers from the decedent's Inter Vivos Trust are paid from the residuary portion of the Trust. As with the Will, the beneficiaries of a specific gift from the Trust are not responsible to pay Estate Taxes on that gift unless there is not enough money left in the Trust to pay for the Estate Taxes.

THE TRANSFER OF THE HOMESTEAD

Under Florida law, if your homestead is inherited by your spouse or descendants according to Florida law (see Chapter 2), then any Estate Tax on that transfer is paid by other beneficiaries of your Estate in the following order:

1st   Beneficiaries of certain Non-probate transfers such as Pay On Death accounts, beneficiary of a life insurance policy, etc.

2nd   If there are no such beneficiaries, or there are not enough funds available from such transfers, then Estate Taxes due on the homestead must be paid from the Residuary Probate Estate or from the residuary portion of the decedent's Inter Vivos Trust.

3rd   If there are insufficient funds in the Residuary Estate of the Will or Trust, then the beneficiaries under the decedent's Will or Trust will need to pay the Estate Taxes on the homestead.
(FS 731.201, 733.817).

The above discussion of the provisions of Florida statute 733.817 is abridged. The statute is some 7 pages long, and contains lots of "but if's." For example, the Personal Representative, or the Trustee of the Inter Vivos Trust, or any beneficiary can ask the Court to decide how much each beneficiary should contribute to the payment of taxes. Such a request is appropriate whenever the burden of paying the taxes falls too heavily on one or more beneficiaries.

Notice that, with the exception of certain Non-probate assets, the residuary beneficiaries of your Will and/or Trust are responsible to pay your Estate Taxes. This means that the amount that your residuary beneficiaries receive will be reduced by the amount of Estate Taxes paid. If this is not as you wish, you can have your Will and/or Trust make other provisions for the payment of your Estate Taxes.

After reading the last few pages you may thinking "Looks like everyone should have a Will." And we would agree with your conclusion. Regardless of whether you arrange for all of your property to pass directly without the need for Probate; and regardless of whether you have a Trust, it is important that you have a Will for all of the reasons just stated.

Anyone who is at least 18 years of age and of sound mind can make a Will (FS 732.501). Courts have ruled that "Sound mind" means that when you made the Will you knew:

☑ what property you owned - and -

☑ who of your relatives would, under ordinary circumstances, expect to inherit your property - and -

☑ you understood the practical effect of the Will, i.e. who would inherit your property under that Will. (*American Red Cross v. Estate of Haynsworth*, 708 So.2d 602 (Fla. 1998).

You may be thinking "That seems simple enough. I think I'll sit down and write one out." But preparing a Will is like figure skating. It is harder than it looks. A Will needs to be clearly worded. A sentence that can be read in two different ways can lead to a dispute over what you intended; and that could lead to a long and expensive Court battle.

Your Will needs to be prepared according to Florida law, and signed in the presence of at least two witnesses, each of whom also signs the Will (FS 732.502).

Under Florida law, you can have a beneficiary of your Will serve as a witness (FS 732.504). However, it is better that you choose someone who has no interest in the Will.

The problem of having a beneficiary present when you sign your Will is one of **undue influence**. Undue influence occurs whenever someone exerts such pressure on the Will maker so that he is not acting according to his own free will. But undue influence is not easily proven. Florida courts have ruled that to prove undue influence, whoever challenges the Will must prove:
⇨   the person who used such pressure was a substantial beneficiary of the Will; and,
⇨   he had a close and confidential relationship with the Will maker; and,
⇨   he was instrumental in having the Will prepared; i.e., the Will was prepared because of his efforts.

If it is proved that the gift was obtained because of undue influence, the Court will consider the gift to be invalid; i.e., the person who used undue influence will not receive that gift (FS 732.5165).

Even if there was no undue influence, and the Will is clearly worded, properly signed and witnessed, it can still be challenged if you are married and did not make proper provision for your spouse. As explained in Chapter 3 your spouse has the right to an Elective Share, which in Florida, is equal to 30% of your Elective Estate (see page 51) (FS 732.2065).

Although your spouse has the right to elect against your Will, your adult child has no such statutory right. You can give your child as much, or as little as you wish. You have the right to give the child nothing at all.

If you are concerned that someone may challenge your Will, it is important that you consult with an attorney who is experienced in Estate Planning. The attorney will prepare the Will according to your wishes. If you meet with the attorney in the privacy of his office, and without anyone else present, it will be difficult to prove that someone was using undue influence to have you make gifts according to their wishes and not yours.

Once the Will is prepared according to your direction, the attorney can supervise the signing of your Will. He will see to it that your Will is signed and witnessed in the presence of two disinterested witnesses — usually members of his staff, and a Notary Public. Each witness will sign the Will next to your name as witness; and they will sign a separate paragraph saying that they saw you sign the Will. The Notary will also sign a paragraph acknowledging that you and the witnesses signed the Will. Once signed in this manner the Will is considered to be *Self-proved* meaning that it can be admitted to Probate without any further testimony from the witnesses as to its authenticity (FS 732.503).

A Will that is prepared and signed in this manner is difficult to challenge. Your attorney will be able to present proof to the Court that the Will was prepared exactly as you wished, and that no one was present to influence you. The attorney and the witnesses to your Will, can testify that you signed the Will willingly and that you were competent to know what you were doing when you signed the Will.

STORING YOUR WILL

Once you sign your Will, you may wonder where to store it. If an attorney prepared your Will, he may suggest that he place it in his vault for safekeeping. By doing so, he ensures that your heirs will need to contact him as soon as you die. This does not mean that they are required to employ him should a Probate procedure be necessary. It only means that he will have an opportunity for future employment.

But there are problems with such an arrangement. The Will could be lost or mistaken for another Will. That happened in at least one case. The attorney prepared Wills for two people with the same name and similar family circumstances. When one person died the attorney submitted the wrong Will to Probate.

If you decide to allow your attorney to store the Will, you need assurance that the attorney will be responsible for the document. You should get a receipt and something in writing that says:

⇨   The attorney accepts full responsibility for storage of the Will. Should it be lost or damaged, he will replace the document at no cost to you; and if you are deceased, he will, at no cost to your heirs, present sufficient evidence to the Court to accept a valid copy of the Will into Probate.

⇨   There will be no charge to you, or your heirs, for the storage and retrieval of the document.

⇨   Should he sell his practice, retire, or die, he or the successor to his practice, will return the original document to you.

THE SAFE DEPOSIT BOX, SAFE BUT . . .

You might consider placing your document in a safe deposit box that you lease at a bank. The only problem with the bank safe deposit box is convenient access. If you hold a safe deposit box in your name only, then should you die, the bank will restrict access to the safe deposit box. Under Florida law, your spouse, child, parent, or person named as Personal Representative of your Will can inspect the contents of your safe box provided they do so under the supervision of a bank employee (FS 655.935). If your Will is there, the bank can forward it to the Probate Court.

Other than your Will, deed to burial plot, and insurance policy, nothing can be removed without Court authority. Once a Personal Representative is appointed by the Court, he will have such authority. He will be able to take possession of the contents of your safe deposit box. But if you arranged your finances to avoid Probate, it is self defeating trigger a Probate procedure just to get the contents of your safe deposit box (655.936, FS 733.6065).

For those who are married, the solution to the problem of accessing the safe deposit box after death, is to lease the box jointly with your spouse, such that each of you has free access to the box. Those who have a Trust can solve the problem by giving their Successor Trustee joint access to the safe deposit box. If you are single and do not have a Trust, you can lease the box jointly with a trusted family member. Of course, if privacy and security are important to you, then that may outweigh any concern for the convenience of your beneficiaries.

Regardless of where you choose to store your Will, let your Personal Representative know that you have a Will and how to retrieve it in the event of your death.

A Will is Not Enough in Florida

I thought you said a Will is not enough

After reading this chapter, you may be thinking that the book is poorly named. After all, look at all the good things a Will can do:

- ❉ choose the person you want to settle your Estate
- ❉ arrange to have your Personal Representative settle your Estate for a reasonable fee
- ❉ give your personal items, including your car, to the person of your choice
- ❉ choose a Guardian for your child
- ❉ discourage a challenge to your Will.

But that is not all there is to an Estate Plan. A Will cares for your property when you are deceased, but it cannot provide for the care of your property in the event you become disabled. A complete Estate Plan provides for the care of your property during your lifetime and for the care of your person as well.

In these days of extended old age, many of us will need assistance with our health care and/or finances as we age. It is important to arrange to have someone manage finances and make medical decisions in the event that we are too aged or too ill to do so ourselves. These topics are covered in Chapters 8 and 9.

And a Will may be effective to transfer all that you own upon your death, but it cannot help your family pay for your debts. It may be that you have so many debts that your family is left with little or nothing. A complete Estate Plan provides for the financial well being of your family once you are deceased; and that is the topic of the next chapter.

Arranging To Pay Bills 5

You can think of your Estate Plan as being composed of two separate parts, a Lifetime Plan and an Inheritance Plan. Your Lifetime Plan provides for the care of your property during your lifetime, with the goal being maximum control and protection. Your Inheritance Plan provides for the inheritance of your property, with the goal of minimum cost and hassle to your beneficiaries. You could consider your Estate Plan to be a master plan that balances the goals of the Lifetime Plan with those of the Inheritance Plan.

When people consider their Inheritance Plan, they are mostly concerned about giving their possessions away. Many do not take into account how the bills they have accumulated will be paid once they are deceased, or even who will be responsible for paying those bills. Most of us do not worry about providing for the payment of our debts, thinking "I'll have that paid off long before I die." But with easily available credit, many are maintaining a high debt balance as a way of life. Paying off all of their loans is not a priority. Many will live their lives without ever being free of debt.

This does not imply that people do not know how to manage their funds. For many people (and corporations), it makes good sense to use other people's money to carry on business. In fact, great debt is a badge of honor for the wealthy. If a bank will lend you a million dollars, it means you have the means to repay that amount. Banks will not lend much money to those with few assets. Rich or poor, we all need to think about how our debts will be paid once we are gone.

Suppose you die without funds, and owing money. Does the debt die with you or is someone else responsible to pay what you owe? If you are married, the first person the creditor will look to, is your spouse. To understand the basis of this expectation, you need to know a bit of the history of our legal system.

Our laws are derived from the English Common Law. Under English Common law, a single woman had the right to own property in her own name and also the right to contract to buy or sell property. When a woman married, her legal identity merged with her spouse. She could not hold property free from her husband's claim or control. She could no longer enter into a contract without her husband's permission.

Once married, a woman became financially dependent on her husband. He, in turn, became legally responsible to provide his wife with basic necessities — food, clothing, shelter and medical services. If anyone provided basic necessities to his wife, then, regardless of whether the husband agreed to be responsible for the debt, he became obliged to pay for them. This law was called the DOCTRINE OF NECESSARIES.

In the United States, a series of Married Women's Rights Acts were passed giving a married woman the right to own property. The Florida law gives a married woman the same right to contract, own property and run a business in the same manner as any single woman (FS 708.08).

As Married Women's Rights laws were passed state to state, a series of cases tested whether the Doctrine of Necessaries still applied in that state.

Questions that judges had to decide were:

If a wife can own property and contract to pay for her own necessities, should her husband be responsible for such debts in the event she does not have enough money to pay for them?

And if the husband is responsible to pay for his wife's necessities should she be responsible for his?

In Florida the answer was "no" to both questions (*Connor vs. Southwest Florida Regional Medical Center, Inc.,* 668 So.2d 175 (Fla. 1995)).

Under current Florida law neither partner is responsible to pay for the necessities of the other. If the spouse who made the contract or purchase, does not have sufficient funds to pay, then his/her spouse is not responsible for the debt unless the spouse agrees to do so.

Which leads to the next question. Is anyone other than your spouse responsible to pay monies you owe? For joint debts, the answer is "yes."

JOINT DEBTS

A *joint debt* is a debt that two or more people are responsible to pay. Usually the contract or promissory note reads that both parties agree to *joint and several* liability, meaning they both agree to pay the debt and each of them, individually, agree to pay the debt. A joint debt can also be in the form of monies owed by one person with payment guaranteed by another person. If the person who owes the money does not pay, then the *guarantor* (the person who guaranteed payment) is responsible to pay the debt.

Should you die, your hospital bills, nursing home bills, funeral expenses, legal fees for the Probate of your Estate, are all debts of your Estate. They are not joint debts unless someone guaranteed payment for the monies owed. Hospital and nursing home bills are considered to be necessaries, so if you are married and there are insufficient funds in the Estate to pay for these bills, then your spouse is responsible for payment, regardless of whether your spouse agreed to be jointly liable for the debt.

JOINT SPOUSAL DEBTS

Your spouse is responsible to pay for loans signed by both of you. For example, if you both are authorized to use a credit card, and there is no money in your Estate, then your spouse must pay the debt. Property taxes are a joint debt if you and your spouse both own the property.

JOINT PROPERTY BUT NO JOINT DEBT

Suppose you own property jointly with another person. If you owe money, can your creditor take your share of the property to pay the monies you owe? This may seem like a simple question, but the answer depends on several factors. First, and most importantly, is how the property is titled. If you own the property as a Tenant In Common, your creditor can take your share of the property to pay the debt. If you own the property together with your spouse as Tenants By The Entirety, your creditor cannot take that property to pay your debt, not during your lifetime and not upon your death, because, as explained on Page 32, each partner own the property 100% both before and after death (*Hurlbert v. Shackleton* 560 So.2d 1276 (Fla.App. 1990)).

Things get complicated if you own the property as Joint Tenants with Right of Survivor, even if the other Joint Tenant happens to be your spouse. Florida Courts have ruled that a creditor can require a Joint Tenant to use his share of the property to pay the debt. However, once the debtor dies, he no longer owns the property, and the creditor cannot force the surviving joint owner to use the property to pay the debt (*D.A.D, Inc. v. Moring, 218 So.2d 451* (Fla.App. 1969)).

JOINT PROPERTY — JOINT DEBT

It's a different story if the other Joint Tenant owes the money as well. For example, if you have a joint account with your son and you have a credit card in both your names. Should one of you die, the other is responsible to pay the bill regardless of who ran up the bill. The bill can be paid from the joint account or from any other account owned by the surviving debtor.

PAYING FOR CREDIT CARD DEBT

Most of us are wise enough not to hold a credit card jointly with a child, but most of us do not hesitate to hold a credit card with our spouse, especially if we are using the card to pay for necessities. If paying that bill could be a struggle for the surviving spouse, you might consider credit card insurance to cover the debt.

Many credit card companies offer insurance policies and include the premium as part of the monthly payment. It benefits the credit card company to offer life insurance as part of the credit package, because they are assured of prompt payment should the borrower die.

Of course, in these days of high credit card interest rates, you and your spouse may be struggling to pay your monthly credit charge. Adding still another charge to the account may not be an option, regardless of the security offered to your spouse. In such case, a better route might be for you to remove your name from the account and open a new account in your name only. This is especially important if you are using your credit card to pay for your business expenses. Your surviving spouse is not responsible to pay for your business debts unless your spouse agreed to do so.

Still another reason not to hold a joint credit card is that each of you can establish your own line of credit in the event one of you retires or is out of work. Should the breadwinner of the family die, it may be difficult for the surviving spouse to establish credit if the spouse is retired and/or has no recent work record. It is easier for an unemployed spouse to establish a line of credit when he/she is married to someone who is working.

OTHER TYPES OF LOAN INSURANCE

Many mortgage companies offer mortgage insurance to their borrowers. Mortgage rates are currently low, so an additional charge for mortgage insurance on the life of the primary wage earner may be worth the effort. This is particularly the case with families raising children. With such insurance, the family can inherit the homestead free of debt. The monthly insurance charge may be a small price to pay to ensure that the children can continue to live in their own home until they are grown.

Car loan insurance is still another thing to consider. If a married couple purchases (or leases) a car, and one of them dies, it may be a struggle for the other to pay off the loan. This was the case with Eva and Howard. Both had to work to support their three children. They owned two well used cars. It seemed that one car or the other was always in the shop. When they saw a NO INTEREST advertisement for a new car, they decided the offer was too good to pass up.

The monthly payments were high, but it was their only luxury. With both their salaries, they were able to make the payments. When Howard had his first heart attack, he was out of work for several weeks so they struggled to keep the payments current. Howard worked in construction, and was anxious to return to work. The doctors advised that such work might be too strenuous for his weakened heart. Construction work was all Howard knew, and the pay was good, so he ignored the warning and went back to his old job.

The second heart attack was fatal, leaving Eva as the sole means of support for her family.

With Howard gone there was no need for two cars. Eva could not afford the payments on the new car anyway, so she decided to sell it. Unfortunately, what she could get for the car was significantly less than the balance owed. Once she fell behind in payments she decided to surrender the car rather than have them repossess it. She was sure they would understand, considering all that she had been through these past several months, not to mention that she was a widow with three small children.

They didn't understand.

The company took the car and then sued for the balance of monies owed. The judge was sympathetic, but under the law there is no "life is tough" defense. He ruled that Eva had to pay the monies owed; and, as per the terms of the loan agreement, she even had to pay the fees for the company's attorney and all court costs. What an emotional and financial nightmare!

The pity was, it all could have been avoided, had they worked payment of debts into their Estate Plan. Howard was the primary driver of the new car and the primary wage earner. All he had to do was to put the loan in his name only, and take out loan insurance. Eva would have inherited the car, debt free. She could have kept it or sold it as she saw fit.

Even if Howard didn't purchase loan insurance, had he put the loan in his name only, the company could only have sued his Estate. They would not have been able to sue Eva personally.

The good part of purchasing loan insurance — be it credit card insurance, mortgage insurance or car insurance, is that you can usually purchase the insurance without taking a medical examination. The down side is that companies generally do not offer such insurance to those over the age of 65; and for those under 65 the cost of the insurance is a factor. It usually costs more to purchase loan insurance than a life insurance policy. Those in fairly good health need to comparison shop. If it is your goal to have insurance cover all of your outstanding debts, then the cost of a single life insurance policy may be much less than purchasing several loan insurance policies.

The Estate Planning strategy of purchasing life insurance to pay off all of your loans works best if you are married and your spouse is jointly liable for your debts. If you name your spouse as beneficiary of the life insurance policy, then he/she can use the life insurance funds to pay off all monies owed. If you name your spouse (or anyone else) as beneficiary of your insurance policy, and that person has no legal obligation to pay your debts, then none of your creditors can ask your beneficiary to use the insurance funds to pay your debts. The only exception is if you purchase an insurance policy to defraud your creditors. If a creditor can prove that you bought the policy rather than pay monies owed to him, a Court can order that whatever you paid for the policy, plus interest, be paid to the creditor from the proceeds of the policy.

If you want the insurance funds used to pay your debts, you need to name your Estate as beneficiary of your policy and your Personal Representative will use those funds to pay any money you owe (FS 222.13).

If you want someone to inherit money after you are gone, and you do not want those funds reduced by the cost of Probate or to pay off your debts, naming that person as beneficiary of the insurance proceeds should accomplish your goal.

With or without debt, you may be wondering about life insurance — should you have it? How much is enough? The answer to these questions depends on the "sleep at night" factor, namely how much insurance do you need so that you won't worry about insurance coverage when you go to sleep at night? It is often more an emotional than a financial issue.

Some people have an "every man for himself" attitude and are content to have no life insurance at all. When they die, whatever they have, they have. And that is what their heirs will inherit. Others worry about how their loved ones will manage if they are not around to support them, and decide to purchase enough insurance to maintain their dependents in their accustomed life style. The same person may have different thoughts about insurance coverage as circumstances change — from no coverage in his bachelor days to more-than-enough coverage in his child rearing days to just-enough-to-bury-me in his senior years.

Insurance companies recognize that people's needs change over the years. Many companies offer flexible insurance coverage. As with any consumer item, it is a good idea to shop around. In addition to the problem of how much life insurance to carry, there is the concern of how the monies will be spent. Leaving a large sum of money to a person who is less than prudent, may lead to a spending spree.

Most beneficiaries go through their inheritance within two years. For many, the reason the money is gone so soon, is that there just wasn't much money to inherit in the first place. But for others, it's a spending frenzy. Luckily, people are fairly consistent in their spending habits, so you probably know in advance whether your intended beneficiary will "go wild," or prudently invest the monies he inherits.

If you want to leave an insurance policy benefit to someone you love, but the intended beneficiary is immature, or a born spendthrift, then a simple solution to the problem may be to purchase an *Annuity* rather than a life insurance policy with a single lump sum payment. You can purchase an Annuity from an insurance company so that upon your death (the *Annuitant*) receives money on a regular basis (monthly, quarterly, yearly) rather than one large payment.

Hopefully, this regular source of income will encourage your beneficiary to think ahead, and learn to budget his finances.

In addition to spreading out the inheritance, you can protect the insurance funds from the claims of the creditors of your beneficiary. In Florida, monies received by your beneficiary under an annuity contract are exempt from the claims of his creditors (FS 222.14). This means that the creditor cannot force the insurance company to pay the annuity to the creditor instead of the beneficiary. Of course, once the beneficiary receives the annuity, he can use some, or all of it to pay monies that he may owe.

THINGS THAT CAN BE INHERITED DEBT FREE

There are certain items that can be inherited by your beneficiary free of the claims of your creditors. As discussed, the beneficiary of your life insurance policy inherits the proceeds of the policy free from the claims of your creditors. And that is so, regardless of the value of the life insurance policy and regardless of whether it was a group insurance policy, a health or accident policy (FS 733.808).

There are other items that can be inherited free of your debts under Florida law

◇ BENEFITS TO TEACHER OR ADMINISTRATOR ◇
The state of Florida provides a death benefit of $75,000 to any teacher or school administrator who is killed in his line of duty as the result of an intentional act of violence. If the teacher has not named a specific beneficiary, then the money is paid to the decedent's Estate. These funds are exempt from the claims of the decedent's creditors (FS 112.1915).

◇ FINAL WAGES ◇
Your employer can pay any wages and travel expenses that are due, directly to your spouse. If there is no spouse, the employer can pay the funds to your adult children; and if no children, then to your parents. All of your wages and up to $300 in travel expenses are taken by any of these family members free of creditor claims. If none of these family members survive you, the funds become part of your Estate and are available to pay your debts (FS 222.15, 222.16).

Annuities, pensions, profit sharing or other retirement plans regulated by the federal Employee Retirement Income Security Act of 1974 ("ERISA"), including IRA accounts and plans identified by the Internal Revenue Code as 401(a) and 403(a & b), 408, 408A and 409 are creditor proof. Monies received by a beneficiary of such plans are protected from the decedent's AND beneficiaries creditors with the following exceptions:

NO EXEMPTION FOR TAXES

In general, income taxes are not paid when money is placed in a retirement plan. Taxes are paid when the monies are withdrawn from the account regardless of whether the monies are withdrawn by the retiree or the person he named as beneficiary of the retirement plan. If your beneficiary inherits money from your pension, retirement allowance, or annuity, he may need to pay taxes on those monies.

NO EXEMPTION FOR QUALIFIED DOMESTIC RELATIONS ORDER

If a Court has ordered the decedent or beneficiary to pay funds to his family under a Qualified Domestic Relations Order, then the pension funds are available to make such payment (FS 222.21).

✧ EXEMPTIONS FOR SURVIVING SPOUSE ✧

Your surviving spouse and/or minor children are entitled to take certain items of your Estate free from the claims of creditors. These rights are available to the surviving spouse, provided he/she did not sign a prenuptial or postnuptial agreement giving up such rights (FS 732.702).

THE HOMESTEAD EXEMPTION ✧

Florida property that was owned and occupied by you as your homestead (i.e. principal residence) is protected from the creditor claims with the exception of taxes, mortgages on the property, or mechanics' liens for work done to the property. This creditor protection continues for the benefit of the surviving spouse or children who inherit the property according to Florida law (see pages 68 and 69) (Florida Constitution, Article X, Section 4).

The Florida Homestead Exemption is unlimited in value. A home could be worth millions of dollars, and the creditors of the homeowner could not reach those funds. There is a bill that has been proposed in the United States Congress, which would, if passed, limit the value of the Homestead Exemption. The amount proposed was $100,000. Should that bill become law, then a creditor could force the sale of the property. The homeowner would be entitled to the first $100,000 of the proceeds of the sale. Anything over that value would be available to the creditor.

As yet, the bill has not become law, so, in Florida, the Homestead Exemption remains unlimited.

EXEMPT PERSONAL PROPERTY ✧

The surviving spouse is entitled to take the following *Exempt Property* free from the decedent's creditor claims, except for monies owed on any given item:

⇨ all automobiles held in the decedent's name and regularly used by the decedent or his family as their personal automobile

⇨ all household furniture, furnishings, and appliances up to $10,000 in value.

⇨ any Florida Prepaid College Program contract

If there is no surviving spouse, the decedent's children inherit these items free from any creditor claim (FS 732.402). If the decedent made a gift of any Exempt item in his Will then it is no longer Exempt Property; however if the gift was made to the surviving spouse; or if no spouse, to his children, then the beneficiary can ask the Court to allow it to keep its Exempt status.

THE FAMILY ALLOWANCE ✧

The decedent's spouse and/or his dependent descendants (children, grandparents, etc.) and/or his parents or grandparents who were dependent on him for support, are entitled to receive a *Family Allowance* for their maintenance during the Probate procedure. Up to $18,000 of the Probate Estate can be paid as a Family Allowance. It can be paid as a single lump sum or it can paid monthly. The Court sets the value of the Family Allowance and to whom it should be paid. The Family Allowance is free from creditor claims, with the exception of monies owed to administer the Estate, funeral and burial expenses, taxes, and the reasonable medical expenses of the last 60 days of the decedent's illness (FS 732.403, 733.707).

AN ESTATE PLAN FOR THE BANKRUPT

You may think the above title to be an oxymoron (a contradiction in terms). If a person is bankrupt, why plan for an Estate he doesn't have? But facts are, that people who file for bankruptcy are often quite wealthy and that is their downfall. Because they have substantial income or property, banks and people are willing to lend them money. If more money is borrowed than can be repaid, the unhappy result is bankruptcy. In the event you are concerned about meeting your responsibilities as parent or spouse, yet you enjoy a life style of financial brinksmanship, then consider investing in items that are "creditor proof."

That's exactly what Alan decided to do. Alan was astute, well aware of his strengths and weaknesses. He enjoyed his work and knew he had the capacity to earn large sums of money. But he also knew he was a gambler. Not the Las Vegas type, but a gambler in business ventures. "No risk, no gain" was one his favorite sayings.

If you charted Alan's net worth over the years it would look like the peaks and valleys of the NASDAQ. Lots of high highs and low lows. Unfortunately, he married a woman who did not share his adventurous spirit. His wife became increasingly intolerant of their financial instability. She came to realize that this was his life style and things would never change. "All gamblers die broke," she said as she walked out the door with their 5 year old daughter in tow.

That, and the fact that he had to declare bankruptcy, brought Alan up short; and he began to be concerned about his future and that of his family.

Alan talked things over with his bankruptcy attorney "I am a good businessman, but not a clairvoyant. There was no way to predict the turn of events that led to this situation. But I know I will bounce back, and it will just be a matter of time before I earn my next fortune. I also know that I am an entrepreneur and not a 9 to 5 type guy so this could happen again. What concerns me is how to provide some security for my child in case something happens to me before she is grown."

"There are many items here in Florida that are creditor proof. Your Homestead Exemption is unlimited. Your daughter can inherit your home free from the claims of your creditors. You could put money into a federal retirement plan such as an IRA or Keogh account, and your daughter would inherit that free of your debts."

Alan didn't think that would work. "I am my own boss, and I don't have the self discipline to put money aside each month for my retirement."

The attorney suggested "If you are concerned about your daughter's education, you could participate in Florida's Prepaid College Trust Fund. The amount you pay each month into the fund depends on the age of your daughter at the time you sign the Prepaid College Fund contract. Under that contract she can go to any college in Florida and her college tuition will be paid. Provided you don't terminate the contract, any money you pay into the Fund is free from the claims of your creditors. It is also free of monies owned by your daughter (FS 222.22). You can also purchase a life insurance policy that could pay for her living expenses during her college years. Your daughter will inherit the proceeds free of your debts. Even the cash surrender value of the policy is creditor proof during your lifetime."

The attorney cautioned "I don't recommend you buy the insurance policy right now. If you purchase the policy when you are insolvent (i.e., you owe more than you own), and then die, your creditors will say that you bought the policy to avoid paying your debts. If the court finds that you bought the policy to defraud your creditors, any money you paid for the policy is available to pay those creditors. But only the premium (what you paid for the policy) is at risk. If the premium is just a small part of the proceeds of the insurance policy, then maybe this is not of concern to you."

Alan mentioned that he had separated from his wife, and was thinking of moving back North.

The attorney did not think that a good idea "There is much creditor protection here in Florida, but many other states have little creditor protection. For example, in New York only $10,000 of the homestead is protected. New Jersey has no homestead creditor protection at all."

Alan was curious "What do people do to protect their assets in those states?"

"Well some — the very wealthy — set up Offshore Trusts."

"How does that work?"

"They put their money into a Trust. When they do so, they essentially give up control of that money."

Alan was skeptical "Oh come now. Why would anyone put his money where he can't get to it?"

The attorney explained "The Trust can be set up so that funds are available for whatever the millionaire wants. Usually funds are made available to support his family. Trust funds can be used to maintain the family home or yacht. Monies from the Trust can be used to pay for travel or for an expensive vacation. And of course the Trust would provide for the transfer of the property to the millionaire's beneficiaries, once the millionaire dies. What the millionaire can't do is be the Trustee of the Trust. The millionaire cannot be Trustee, because if he were, he would have control over the money, and his creditors could take legal action here in the United States to force him to use his Trustee powers to use that money to pay his creditors."

"How can they force the issue? Why couldn't he, as Trustee, just refuse?"

"Remember, that as long as the millionaire is a citizen of the United States, and he is physically present in the states, he is subject to the laws of this country. If a creditor goes to Court and wins, the U. S. Judge could order the millionaire, as Trustee, to use Trust funds to pay that debt. If the millionaire-Trustee refused, the Judge could put him in jail for contempt of Court. No, for an Offshore Trust to work, the Trust must be a foreign Trust, that is, drafted according to the laws of a foreign country, Trust property must be located outside of the United States, and the Trustee cannot be a citizen of the United States."

Alan said "Well I guess the millionaire might have a relative who is not a U.S. citizen to manage the Trust."

The attorney agreed "Yes, or he could use a financial institution that does not do business in the U.S., to manage the funds. But there are other problems with an Offshore Trust. There's the safety factor. Trust funds are kept outside of the United States. If the funds are kept in a foreign bank and the country suffers an economic collapse, then those funds could be lost."

Alan wondered "Isn't that much the same risk as money in a U.S. bank? Only $100,000 of the cash in a U.S. bank account is insured. If the bank fails, any money in that bank over $100,000 could be lost."

The attorney disagreed "Our U.S government is stable, and we trust that they will regulate U.S. banks and keep our money safe. But that is not the case with other small countries. The government of a small country could collapse and the banks along with it."

"But why keep money in a bank? Most millionaires have their funds invested in stocks and bonds, or in real property."

The attorney agreed "True, but real estate could be risky. If your Trust contains real property located within the United States, your creditor could go to a U.S. court and take that property."

Alan wondered "Couldn't the creditor take the overseas property as well?"

"He could, but it would be hard. For one thing he would need to find the property. And the Trustee is not about to tell him where it is, unless the creditor sues, and the laws of that foreign country require the Trustee to tell. Even if the creditor locates Trust property, whether it is stocks, bonds, or real estate, most Offshore Trusts are established in countries that are not creditor friendly. For example, if you set up an off shore Trust in the Cook Islands, they will not accept a judgment that a creditor got in the United States. The creditor will need to employ a Cook Islands attorney to sue you all over again in the Cook Islands. That's expensive. And the Cook Islands have a higher standard of proof. Here in the U.S., all your creditor need do is to show that you owe the money *by a preponderance of the evidence.* That's lawyer talk for "the jury must be more than 50% sure you owe the money." In the Cook Islands, the creditor's attorney must prove you owe the money *beyond a reasonable doubt* (Cook Islands, International Trusts Act of 1984 Section 13B(1)). That standard is the one we use here in the U.S. for criminal cases. In addition, the foreign country usually has a short Statute of Limitations, so if your creditor does not sue you in that country within that period of time, he cannot sue you at all."

Alan said "I can see why Offshore Trusts are so popular."

The attorney cautioned "But there are other problems. The U.S. considers transfers into and/or out of the Trust to be taxable. The IRS requires special tax returns to be filed for all foreign Trusts. In addition, the IRS looks closely at Offshore Trusts to determine whether they are fraudulent transfers, designed to avoid U.S. income taxes or U.S. Estate taxes. The IRS wants to be sure that the creditor the millionaire is avoiding isn't Uncle Sam!"

Alan said "Yes, but if you pay your taxes, that shouldn't be a problem. If I ever get to the point where I am that wealthy, then I'll come back and discuss setting up an Offshore Trust."

The attorney refused "No, I'm just a country lawyer. If you want to go that route, you need a specialist — someone who has overseas connections, and who has experience in writing such Trusts. If you are serious about setting up an Offshore Trust, let me know and I will recommend someone to you."

"O.K. I will."

The attorney offered a final word of caution "If you are able to accumulate a significant amount of money, don't risk it all in a business venture. Limit the amount of money you can lose to just the money that you invest in business. Keep your personal funds separate and protected from your business debts. If you want to start a business, make sure that you cannot be personally liable for your business debts. You can avoid personal liability by forming a corporation, or a Limited Partnership, or a Limited Liability Company.** Stay away from a sole proprietorship or a business partnership."

** These topics are discussed in the next chapter.

Your Business Estate Plan 6

It would take a very thick book to do justice to the topic of Business Estate Planning. Estate Planning issues must be discussed for each type of business:

CONTROL How to control and protect your business during your lifetime.

BENEFICIARY How to be sure your business goes to the beneficiary of your choice.

COST How to transfer your business to your beneficiary quickly and at lowest cost.

With just one chapter to devote to the topic, we can only provide the reader with an overview of the subject. Hopefully, the overview will give the reader some ideas that can later be pursued with a financial planner, or an attorney.

We have written this chapter for the reader who listed a business value as part of his Net Worth on page 4. People who are self employed, but who do not think of themselves as business owners, may profit from the information covered in this chapter, as well.

This chapter should also be of interest to someone who has the possibility of inheriting a business interest, such as the child of a small business owner, or perhaps the spouse of someone who is self employed. Even those who are thinking of starting a business, may find it worthwhile to take a few minutes to read this chapter.

Those who have no present business interest may want to skip this chapter and go on to Chapter 7.

Your business is your property, and as such it is included as part of your overall Estate Plan. But owning a business isn't as simple as just holding title to a tangible item such as a car or parcel of real estate. For example, if you own a business in your name only, i.e. as a *sole proprietor*, there may be no single document that indicates ownership of your business property. You may have filed a Notice of Fictitious Name in your county giving the name of your business and identifying you as the owner of the business; but that does not identify business property. You could have a truck, computers, copiers or other expensive business equipment. Title to that property is probably in your own personal name.

The business bank account may be in your name only, or in the name of the business with you alone as signatory on the account. Charge cards and business loans are either in your name only, or your name as guarantor.

If you want to leave your business to your son, how do you do it? Do you leave him the equipment used in the business? If you are doing business in your name and not a registered Fictious Name, how do you give him that name? And how do you handle business related loans? If you leave him the business, will he agree to be responsible for any outstanding business debt?

Partnerships can be even more complicated, unless there is a written partnership agreement that says how the business is to be transferred in the event that one of the partners dies. Even the transfer of a corporation can be a major headache if there are several shareholders and no shareholders' agreement to say how shares should be transferred in the event of the death or incapacity of the shareholder.

For these reasons, it is important to think about an Estate Plan for your business. You need to ask yourself:

How can I have maximum protection and control over my business during my lifetime?

How can I structure my business so that it can be transferred quickly and at minimum cost?

We will examine each type of business ownership as it relates to the above questions.

WHAT'S THE BEST TYPE OF BUSINESS OWNERSHIP?

Those who read the first five chapters know us well enough not to expect a definitive answer to the above question. Our job, as we see it, is to explain the rules of the game (i.e., Florida law) to the reader. Once you know how things work in Florida, you can make an informed decision as to the type of business ownership that best accomplishes your goal.

> ### SOLE PROPRIETORSHIP
> Maximum control — Maximum liability

You are the boss if you do business in your name only, but you take full personal responsibility for any loss suffered by the company; and as explained, you may need to consult with an attorney if you want to make arrangements for someone to take over your business should you become incapacitated or die.

Because of this personal liability issue, many people think it best to form a corporation as soon as they start up the business. That may not be the best strategy. It takes money to form a corporation. You may need to pay an attorney to set up the corporation. You will need to pay a filing fee to the Florida Secretary of State. Each year you need to file an annual report and pay an annual filing fee. Each year you will need to file separate corporate income tax returns (FS 607.0122, 607.1622).

You do not need to pay filing fees to the Secretary of State to form a sole proprietorship, and you do not need to file separate income tax returns. You can include your business income as part of your personal income tax return and not go through the cost and hassle of filing a separate corporate return.

Another reason to start business as a sole proprietorship is the risk of failure. Although every new business owner thinks his venture must surely culminate in riches, research conducted by the Brandow Company shows that only 55% of new businesses get to celebrate their third birthday (see their data at www.brandow.com). You can always form a corporation should your business succeed. If the business does not succeed, then at least you didn't waste time, effort and money to form a corporation.

But What About My Personal Liability?
Many people seek to limit their personal liability by forming a corporation, however, that doesn't always work in the real world. For example, if you wish to rent a store front or office space, an experienced landlord will allow you to lease the space in the corporate name, but he will require you to sign as a guarantor. Should the business fail, he will have the right to sue you, personally, for the full value of the lease. Once you have established a successful business, the landlord may agree to just hold the business liable; and in that case having a corporation instead of a sole proprietorship will limit your personal liability.

Regardless of what form of business ownership you choose, you can be held personally liable for any fraudulent or negligent act that you commit. The way to avoid personal liability for fraudulent acts is not to willfully (deliberately) deceive or cheat anyone. Most of us are honest folk, but negligence is another matter. We all make mistakes.

The way to limit your liability for negligence is to purchase insurance that provides protection for mistakes and accidents. For example, if you open a title insurance business, you can purchase an Errors and Omissions insurance policy to cover a loss caused by a mistake you might make in a title search. If you have any business involving the care of a person (adult or child day care center, nurse practitioner, etc.), it is important to have coverage for an injury to a client due to accident or malpractice.

If you have a business location (a storefront or office) consider purchasing a comprehensive business insurance policy to cover injury to anyone who visits your business, as well as damages to the premises. For example, if you open a flower shop you can get insurance to cover an injury to a customer who slips and falls. The same policy can cover vandalism to your shop, such as a broken plate glass window. You can be compensated for loss should a storm cause the electricity to go out and your shipment of fresh cut flowers wilt for lack of refrigeration.

The purpose of any business insurance policy is to shift the risk of a business loss from your pocket to that of the insurance company.

And the downside is . . .

The problem with insurance is the greater the risk, the greater the cost. We all would like 100% insurance coverage, but few of us can afford the premium. What holds true for life insurance holds true for business insurance. The right amount of insurance coverage for you is the amount that allows you to sleep at night.

A business partnership is much like a marriage. You can both start out with the best of intentions, only to find that you are hopelessly incompatible. The break-up of a business partnership can be just as bitter and hotly contested as the breakup of a marriage. A properly drafted Partnership Agreement is a must — not only to set the terms of a dissolution, but to clearly state what is expected of each partner; i.e., how much each will contribute to the business venture in terms of effort or financing.

The Partnership Agreement should cover what will happen to the partner's share in the event of his incapacity or death. Most Partnership Agreements provide for an appraisal of the business and the buy out of the deceased (or disabled) partner's share. The Partnership Agreement may need to be backed up with financing. For example, you could sign a Partnership Agreement that requires the company to buy out your partnership interest should you become disabled or die. But what good is the Agreement if there is not enough cash in the company to pay for the buy out?

You will have better protection if the Partnership Agreement requires the company to maintain disability and life insurance to pay for the buy out. Many insurance companies offer Key man insurance. The policy is designed to compensate the company for the loss of someone who is essential to the continuation of the business. If sufficient insurance is purchased, the proceeds of the policy can be used to cover any loss suffered by the company and to buy out the share of the company that was owned by the deceased or disabled partner.

The sole proprietorship and the partnership are the earliest type of business organization. Florida laws governing these types of business organizations have their roots in English Common Law. Common law requires the sole proprietor and each business partner to take full personal responsibility for the debts of the company. As people became ever more litigious (lawyer talk for "sue happy") businessmen sought to limit their liability and prevailed on the legislature to create a form of business ownership to limit that liability.

Legislatures in each state responded to that need by giving businessmen the right to create a company (the corporation) with an identity separate from the owners of the business. By doing business as a corporation, the businessman's liability is limited to the money he invests in the company. A person can sue the corporation for business debts, but not the owners of the corporation.

This does not mean that a corporate owner can use the corporation to do things that are fraudulent. If he does, he can be held personally liable. The owner of the corporation cannot use the corporation as a "veil" to cover his wrongdoing. Florida courts have ruled that they have authority to "pierce the corporate veil" and hold shareholders, officers and directors personally liable whenever justice demands that they be held accountable for using the corporation to do wrongful acts such as defrauding creditors, hiding assets, evading the law, or betraying a trust (*Brooks v. St. John's Motor Sales*, 84 So.2d 1237).

THE CORPORATION
flexible control — limited liability

Whoever forms a corporation (the *incorporator*) has maximum control over the corporation. He decides how the company will operate by having the Articles of Incorporation and the company By-laws prepared according to his specifications. He can keep full control of the company as the only shareholder, or he can distribute shares and give up as much control as he wishes. Transferring corporate ownership is simple. It is a matter of signing a stock certificate transferring the shares of stock in the company. You can have a Transfer On Death designation to a named beneficiary.

If you own shares of stock in your name only, without a TOD designation, your Personal Representative will transfer the shares according to your Will, or if no Will, according to the Laws of Intestate Succession. That may not be the best way to go. If Probate is necessary, it may take several months before the shares are transferred to the proper beneficiary, meanwhile, someone needs to continue to operate the business. If you do not leave specific directions for the continuance of the business, the Personal Representative (or the Probate Court) may decide it best to just sell the company and give the proceeds of the sale to your beneficiaries.

The better route is to have your attorney prepare a Revocable Living Trust and transfer the shares into the Trust. The Trust document can give your Successor Trustee specific instructions about how the business is to be managed or transferred should you become incapacitated or die. Still another important benefit is to avoid the need to Probate what may be your only valuable asset.

THE LIMITED PARTNERSHIP

Just as a sole proprietor can limit his liability by forming a corporation, the partners of a general partnership can limit their liability by converting the partnership to a *Limited Partnership*. As with the corporation, the Limited Partnership is a creation of the legislature and is regulated by Florida law. The name of the Limited Partnership must identify it as a limited partnership or contain the word "Limited" or the abbreviation "Ltd." A Certificate of Limited Partnership must be filed with the Florida Department of State (FS 620.103, 620.108).

The structure of a Limited Partnership differs from a general partnership. In a general partnership, each partner has full authority to conduct business on behalf of the partnership. Each partner is personally liable for monies owed by the partnership, regardless of whether that partner actually incurred the debt. The Limited Partnership has General Partners and Limited Partners. A General Partner has full authority to conduct partnership business and is fully responsible to pay all company debts. A Limited Partner is not liable for company debts unless he participates in the control of the business (FS 620.125, 620.129).

But even a General Partner can avoid personal liability by forming a corporation, and then letting the corporation serve as the sole General Partner. An unpaid creditor of the Limited Partnership can sue the corporate General Partner, but not the shareholders of the corporation. Liability can be limited to the amount of money invested in the business venture. None of the owners will have personal liability. Of course, as with the corporation, all parties can be held personally liable for fraudulent or criminal acts performed in their partnership capacity.

The astute reader might be wondering "Why would anyone form a corporation (and pay all of the costs to set up the corporation) and then make the corporation the General Partner of a Limited Partnership (after paying all that money to set up the Partnership)? If limited business liability is the goal, why not just form a corporation?"

Answers to those questions are many and in fact, far removed from the original goal of limiting the business risk of the partners to just the money they invested in the business. The Limited Partnership can be used as a means of transferring a family business to the children with some significant tax benefits. For example, suppose Mom & Pop run a small, highly profitable, rapidly expanding, gourmet chocolate shop. They have two children, both in college. Right now, the business is worth about $500,000, but they figure that by the time they retire, the business could be worth millions. If their children inherit the business at that time, there could be significant Estate Taxes due. Also, because they are making lots of money right now, they are paying very high income taxes.

Both problems can be solved with a Family Limited Partnership. Mom and Pop can be the General Partners of the company and retain total control. They could make each child a Limited Partner by transferring shares of the business worth less than the current Annual Gift Tax Exclusion. That exclusion is currently $11,000, so together Mom and Pop can gift shares of the partnership up to $22,000 per child, per year. By gifting a percentage of the business each year, the parents can eventually transfer all of the business to the children. When the parents die, there will be no Gift or Estate Tax because the children already own the business. Of course there is still the problem of the Capital Gains Tax should the children decide to sell the business.

Regardless of how much of the company they give away, Mom and Pop can keep total control of the company because they are the General Partners. When the parents are ready to retire, one or both of the children can take over as General Partner — but if making chocolate is not their thing, the parents can arrange to have a corporation manage the Limited Partnership and the children continue to receive income as limited partners. As for the current income tax problem, the children, as Limited Partners, are entitled to receive income from the business. Income paid to the children and their parents is generally taxed at a lower rate than the taxes to just Mom and Pop. For example, suppose the company earns $100,000. Mom and Pop will pay a high rate of income tax if they are the only two partners in the company. If the children become partners, then each partner can earn $25,000 and the overall bill for income taxes will be smaller.

Still another important advantage of the Family Limited Partnership over the corporation is creditor protection for the children's partnership interest. For example, suppose one of the children, becomes a dentist, gets sued for malpractice, and loses the case. If Mom and Pop had incorporated the business and given the children most of the shares of stock in the company, the creditor could take the shares to satisfy the judgment. The creditor could wind up owning the company! Not so, with a Limited Partnership interest. A judge could order that the income from the Limited Partnership be used to pay the judgment, but he could not order the Partnership share itself to be given to the creditor unless the Limited Partnership Agreement allows for such transfer or all Partners agree (FS 620.152, 620.153, 620.154). Not likely with Mom and Pop as General Partners. They might even decide to pay the income to themselves and not distribute anything to the hapless creditor!

We used an actual business as an example to explain how the Limited Partnership worked. It didn't take Estate Planning attorneys long to figure out that the "family business" could be just income producing items (such as stocks and bonds) that Mom and Pop placed into the Limited Partnership. The family "business" could be just the business of earning income. In other words, the Family Limited Partnership (or even a Family Partnership) could just be a type of an Estate Plan created solely for the purpose of transferring assets to the children to avoid paying Estate Taxes, and to pay less in income taxes.

It didn't take the IRS long to challenge this method of Estate Planning. A series of IRS rulings and court cases followed, with the main issue being whether a bona fide business partnership existed.

There is a common sense rule of evidence that says "If it looks like a duck and walks like a duck, and quacks like a duck, it must be a duck." In 1946 the Supreme Court decided that whether a family partnership is really a business partnership for tax purposes, should be determined on a case by case basis; and that the IRS should use the "walk and quack" test. Only the justices said this in proper legal terms. They said to determine whether a partnership exists depends on ". . .whether the partners really and truly intended to join together for the purpose of carrying on a business and sharing in the profits or losses or both. And their intention in this respect is a question of fact, to be determined from testimony disclosed by their agreement, considered as a whole, and by their conduct in execution of its provisions" (*Commissioner v. Tower*, 327 U.S. 280 (1946)).

THE LIMITED LIABILITY COMPANY

The IRS continues to take a close look at family partnerships, and will challenge any tax break if the family partnership (limited or not) does not meet the basic requirement of being a bona fide business partnership. Perhaps in response to IRS challenges, in the 1990s each of the 50 states, and even the District of Columbia, passed laws enabling the residents of their state to form a new business entity called a *Limited Liability Company* ("LLC").

This new entity is not required to be a profit making venture. In Florida, it can be formed for any lawful purpose. A Florida LLC is formed by filing Articles of Organization with the Florida Department of State (FS 608.403, 608.4081)

The LLC combines the better features of the Limited Partnership and the Corporation. Like the corporation, it can be formed by a single person who sets the rules of the company when he forms the corporation. The set of rules is called an *Operating Agreement*. Members who join the company must agree to act in accordance with the Operating Agreement.

The LLC can be run by a manager (who is not a member of the company) or it can be run by a member or members of the company. As with a corporation, all members have limited liability, regardless of whether that member happens to be managing the company. As with a Limited Partnership, a creditor cannot take possession or control of a share of the company owned by a member. The most the creditor can do is get a court to assign income generated by that share to the creditor (FS 608.422, 608.432).

Now Mom and Pop can form a LLC, give away some or all of the shares of the company during their lifetime, and still keep control of the company, and with no more personal liability than a non-managing member of the Limited Liability Company.

Transfers into the Limited Liability Company can be made so that there are no Estate or Gift Tax consequences. Income can be distributed to the children, or not, as Mom and Pop see fit.

The skeptic is probably thinking "Maximum control, limited liability, easily transferred to my beneficiaries, no Estate Tax. This is too good to be true. There must be a catch somewhere."

And so there is. It's called the Capital Gains Tax. If you transfer property during your lifetime, that property is valued by the IRS as of the date of transfer. If you gift a share of the Limited Liability Company during your lifetime, your beneficiary will take your basis in the property (i.e., the value that you paid for your interest in the Company). If you sell the share to your beneficiary, then his basis is the fair market value of the share as of the date of purchase. Either way, once the beneficiary decides to sell the property, there may be a significant Capital Gains Tax due.

An experienced Estate Planning attorney should be able to suggest any number of ways to solve the problem, including purchasing life insurance to pay the tax.

Regardless of what form of business ownership you have, you need to think about what will happen to your business in the event of your incapacity or death. And in particular, how company debts will be paid. If your business is highly leveraged (business talk for "owes lots of money"), you also need to consider how those loans will be paid should you become disabled or die. One solution is to purchase Key man insurance. As explained earlier, Key man insurance is protection for the company against the loss of a valuable employee. The company purchases the policy and the proceeds are paid to the company to compensate it for the loss; but ultimately the policy benefits those who inherit the business.

Taxes are still another concern. Your business may be worth millions on paper, and your Estate Taxes will be based on that value. Your heirs might be forced to sell the company just to pay the taxes, but without your leadership they may get only a fraction of the value of the company.

Even if the federal government decides to eliminate federal Estate Taxes, the state of Florida, or any other state where you have a business location, may decide to levy an Estate or Inheritance Tax.

And there is still the problem of the Capital Gains Tax. No one in Congress is talking about doing away with the Capital Gains Tax — and that tax could be sizeable. One solution to the problem of an unknown Estate Tax and/or Capital Gains Tax is to purchase life insurance that can be used to pay for any Estate Tax that may be due upon your death and any Capital Gains Tax that may be due when your beneficiary sells the property he inherits.

That may sound like a good simple solution, but you need to think things through before calling your insurance agent. The first question being:

How much insurance should I purchase?

That is a tough question. If you are in good health, who knows what will happen before you die. Will your business increase in value or go bust? Will the federal government really do away with Estate Taxes or will they do nothing and allow the tax to be reinstated in 2011?

The last question is particularly troublesome. Under today's tax law, if you purchase a life insurance policy, or even control the benefits of the policy, all of the proceeds of the policy will be counted as part of your taxable Estate. You may be buying insurance just to pay more in taxes to Uncle Sam.

You don't need a soothsayer or psychic to solve the problem. A financial planner with access to computer generated models can predict your life expectancy, how much your business will be worth when you retire and even the probability that the economy will require Estate taxes to be reinstated!

Suppose your financial planner predicts that Estate taxes will be reinstated and that your heirs will probably need to pay 1 million dollars. If you purchase a million dollar insurance policy, the value of the policy will be included in your Estate. If there is an Estate Tax of 40% your heirs will net only $600,000 of your million dollar policy, the rest going for Estate taxes on the proceeds of the policy itself.

Your heirs will need to come up with an additional $400,000 to make up for the original million dollars predicted as being necessary to pay your Estate taxes. The solution to this dilemma is the IRREVOCABLE LIFE INSURANCE TRUST.

THE IRREVOCABLE LIFE INSURANCE TRUST

An *Irrevocable Life Insurance Trust* can be designed to provide money to pay any tax that may be due after your death. To be sure that the IRS does not count the proceeds of the Trust as part of your taxable Estate the Trust must meet the following requirements:

⇨ The Trust must be irrevocable.

⇨ You cannot be Trustee.

The Trust can be set up for the benefit of your child. In such case, the child can be Trustee of the Trust. The child, as Trustee, will purchase an insurance policy on your life. If you give the child a large sum of money to purchase the policy, then you may need to file a Gift Tax return. It is better to give the child $11,000 a year and have the child purchase a policy that is paid with quarterly or annual premiums instead of a single lump sum payment. If you are married, you and your spouse can gift up to $22,000 per year without the need to file a Gift Tax return.

As tax laws change, the child/Trustee can use as much of the gift as is needed to purchase sufficient insurance to cover the taxes. The Trust can be set up to cover Estate taxes or Capital Gains taxes, or both. For example, the Trustee can purchase an insurance policy that pays a million dollars upon your death. Those insurance funds can be used to pay your Estate taxes. Should it happen that no Estate taxes are due, the Trustee can keep the monies invested until the business is sold. The Trust funds can be used to pay any Capital Gains Tax that may be due at that time. If monies are left over once all taxes are paid, they can be distributed to the named beneficiaries of the Trust.

Your attorney can design an Irrevocable Insurance Trust in any number of ways to meet the special needs of you and your family. For example, an Irrevocable Insurance Trust can be set up to solve problems described in the last Chapter. Alan wanted to leave insurance proceeds for his child but was concerned that the cash value of the policy could be taken by his creditors. A properly drafted Irrevocable Insurance Trust can solve such problem, because the Trust, and not Alan, is the owner of the policy.

Of course, it costs significant money to set up and maintain an Irrevocable Insurance Trust. Those who do not have concerns about creditors may wonder whether it's necessary to go through all that cost and bother if there will be no more Estate taxes in the future. After all a simple life insurance policy can cover any Capital Gains Tax that may be due. But, as explained, the tax law as passed in 2001 reinstates the Estate Tax in 2011. If lawmakers take no further action, the Estate of anyone who dies on January 1, 2011, and thereafter is subject to an Estate Tax for an Estate over one million dollars.

Someone with an active imagination could envision the following scenario:

It is New Year's eve, 2010. A 97 year old lies sleeping, at his home, surrounded by his four grandchildren who are his sole heirs.

"He looks so peaceful."

"Yes. Surprising, considering that he has terminal cancer, failing kidneys and heart. His doctor says he can't last more than a few days. The doctor left a supply of morphine so that we can keep Gramps comfortable over the New Year's holiday. The doctor gave him a shot just before he left."

"The doctor said not to give Gramps another shot unless he was in pain. His heart is in such a weakened condition, he could easily overdose on morphine."

"Yes, of course."

"Too bad he didn't get a chance to do some Estate Planning before he had that stroke last year. "

"I thought his attorney took care of all that."

"His attorney suggested he set up an Irrevocable Insurance Trust to pay for any Estate Tax, but Gramps felt sure that Congress would pass a law that would permanently repeal the Estate Tax."

"I can't imagine Gramps coming to that conclusion. The economy is down and the government needs to raise taxes. It is easier for legislators to leave the law as written back in 2001, than take some affirmative action."

"Gramps was always a sharp business man, but in his later years his mind wasn't as clear as when he earned his five million dollars."

"Is that what we are going to inherit?"

"Not unless he dies before midnight. After midnight the Estate Tax is reinstated, and at a rate of 45%. Between state and federal taxes, we'll be lucky to come away with half a mill each."

"Gramps moved. I think he may be in pain."

"Yes, he does look uncomfortable."

"It isn't right to let him suffer like this."

"Yes, of course."

Continuing To Care 7

There are any number of reasons that people give for wanting to continue on with their lives. For the lucky ones, their main reason for living is that they are having a great time and don't want it to end. For many, it is more a sense of responsibility. During child rearing years the concern of the parent is what will happen to the child should the parent suddenly die. Once a child is grown, the roles often reverse, and it is the child worrying about what will happen to his parent if the child were not present to see to the care of the aging parent. Even pet lovers worry about what will happen to their pet should the owner no longer be around.

There is little that can be done to prepare those who depend on you for the loss of your companionship and emotional support; but there are many things you can do to provide financial support for those who rely on you. Even people of modest means can make financial provision so their loved ones will have an easy transition from being dependent to becoming self sufficient.

This chapter explains the many simple, and relatively inexpensive, things you can do to provide care for your loved ones should you not be present to do so yourself.

CARING FOR THE MINOR CHILD

It doesn't happen very often, but both parents could die or become incapacitated before their child reaches adulthood. Most parents don't want to think about, much less prepare for such a happening. But in this age of postponing parenthood, many parents are in their fifties and sixties and still raising children. The probability of a life threatening illness increases with age, so parents need to understand the importance of planning ahead.

Parents with dangerous occupations also need to provide for the care of their minor child in event of the disability or death of both parents. It is surprising to think of how many of us are employed in dangerous occupations. Construction workers, military personnel, firemen, Florida and federal law enforcement agents, and in this day and age, even postal workers face hazards on a daily basis.

Regardless of the parent's age or occupation, planning for the care of a minor child should be part of every parent's Estate Plan, not only because it is the responsible thing to do, but also because it is relatively simple and inexpensive to do.

A child must be cared for in two ways, the *person* of the child and the *property* of the child. To care for the person of the child, someone must be in charge of the child's everyday living, not only food and shelter but to provide social, ethical and religious training. Someone must have legal authority to make medical decisions and see to the child's education. To care for the child's property, someone must be responsible to see that monies left to the child are used for the care of the child and that anything left over is preserved until the child becomes an adult.

A Guardian will need to be appointed to care for the person and property of the child in the event that both parents become incapacitated or die before the child is grown.

USING A WILL TO APPOINT A GUARDIAN

As explained in Chapter 4, each parent can name someone in his Will to serve as Guardian of their minor child. It is a good idea for both parents to name the same Guardian in their respective Wills because should the parents die simultaneously, their nomination will not be effective. If different Guardians are named, it will be up to the Judge to decide who is best suited for the job. If they do not die simultaneously, the Court will give top priority to the person named in the Will of the last parent to die.

One problem with using a Will to appoint someone to be your child's Guardian, is that it may take time for the appointment to be effective. The Court must determine whether the Will is valid; and the person you chose as Guardian needs to file a petition to be appointed as the child's Guardian. It might take several weeks before that person has the legal authority to care for the child.

A better solution is to appoint someone as a *Preneed Guardian* who can immediately assume responsibility for the care of the minor child, should the need arise. The parents can make the appointment by signingaDECLARATION OF PRENEED GUARDIAN.

APPOINTING A PRENEED GUARDIAN

Under Florida law, the parents of a minor child may appoint someone to be their child's Guardian in the event they both become incapacitated or die. The appointment is made by signing a ***Declaration of Preneed Guardian*** in the presence of two witnesses. Both parents must sign the Declaration, however only one signature is necessary in the event that one of the parents is deceased.

The Declaration of Preneed Guardian is a simple document. It can be prepared by the couple's attorney or the parents can prepare one themselves by using a preprinted form or by looking up Florida Statute 744.3046 and preparing the document in conformity with the statute. The statute requires the Declaration to identify the parents and the Preneed Guardian. This is done by giving their names and addresses. The Declaration must contain the name, date of birth and social security number of each minor child named in the Declaration. The parents can name an alternate Preneed Guardian, in the event the person of their choice is unable to take over as the child's Guardian. Once the Declaration is properly signed and witnessed, it needs to be filed with the Clerk of the Circuit Court in the county where the couple reside. The Clerk will keep the Declaration on file until all of the children have reached 18 years of age.

Should both parents become incapacitated or die while the child is a minor, the person they appointed as Preneed Guardian can immediately take over the child's care. Within 20 days, the Preneed Guardian must ask the Court to appoint him as the child's legal Guardian. The Clerk will give the Declaration to the Judge at that time. The Judge will appoint the Preneed Guardian to serve as the child's Guardian unless, for some reason, he determines that person is not qualified for the job.

Many parents never get around to appointing a Guardian because they cannot come to an agreement as to the best choice of Guardian. "I think my mother should be Guardian. After all she raised me, and I turned out fine" can signal the opening salvo of a lengthy, and often un-resolved battle.

Not being able to agree on a choice of Guardian should not discourage you from appointing the person of your choice either as part of your Will or in a separate writing. The thing to keep in mind is that the Guardian of your choice will take over only if the other parent is deceased or incapacitated. Even if you both die simultaneously, and you each name someone different to serve as Guardian, your choice of Guardian will at least be brought to the attention of the Court.

It is important that the person you choose to serve as Guardian be compatible with the child. If your choice of Guardian is not that of the child's, the child can object to the appointment. If the child is at least 14, the Court will listen carefully to the child's objection, and then appoint a Guardian based on the what the Court determines to be in the child's best interest (FS 744.312).

LEAVING PROPERTY FOR THE CHILD

As any parent is well aware, it is expensive to raise a child. The person you consider to be the best choice to serve as Guardian might not be able to do so unless you leave sufficient monies to pay for the care of the child. If you have limited finances, consider purchasing a term life insurance policy on your life and/or on the life of the other parent of the child. If you can only afford one policy, insure the life of the parent who contributes most to the support of the child.

Term insurance policies are relatively inexpensive if you limit the term to just that period of time until your child becomes an adult. Some companies offer a combination of term life and disability insurance, in the event that the bread-winner becomes disabled and unable to work. As with any other purchase, it is important to comparison shop to obtain the best price for the coverage.

If you are married, you may want to name your spouse as the beneficiary of the term insurance policy with your child as an alternate beneficiary. Married or single, you can name your child as the primary beneficiary of the policy. Under Florida law, the insurance company may give amounts up to $10,000 to the child by transferring the funds to whomever has custody of the child. The company is required to seek Court permission to transfer funds to a minor in excess of that amount (FS 710.108).

If the sum to be transferred is substantial Court will probably require that a Guardian of the property be appointed to protect the funds until the child reaches 18.

We discussed the ways parents can control who is appointed to serve as the Guardian of their minor child should both parents be incapacitated or deceased. Guardianship is a necessity in such cases. But if at least one of the parents is able to care for the person of the child, it may be wise to avoid the need for the Court to appoint a Guardian of the property. If you leave the child a significant amount of money the Court will appoint a Guardian of that property. Even if the surviving parent is appointed to serve as Guardian, the amount you leave to the child will be reduced by the cost of establishing and maintaining the guardianship.

An attorney must be employed to establish the guardianship. Once appointed, the Guardian has many duties. He must prepare an inventory and file an annual accounting with the Court. The Guardian may need to employ an accountant to assist with the preparation of the inventory and the annual accounting. Depending on the size of the Estate, the Guardian of the property may need to employ a financial advisor to manage the property. All these fees are proper charges to the child's guardianship property (FS 744.361, 744.367).

Monies left for the care of the child may be significantly reduced by the cost of caring for the property. This can be avoided by leaving property to the child in such a manner, that will make it unnecessary for the Court to appoint a Guardian of the property of the child. One way to do so is to include a Trust for the child as part of your Will. Another is to set up a Revocable Living Trust that includes provisions for the care of the child. If you have limited finances, a good alternative is to appoint someone to serve as Custodian of the gift under the FLORIDA UNIFORM TRANSFERS TO MINORS ACT.

THE UNIFORM TRANSFERS TO MINORS ACT

The *Florida Uniform Transfers to Minors Act* is designed to protect gifts made to a minor by appointing someone to be the *Custodian* of a gift until the child is an adult. For example, you can make a minor child the beneficiary of your life insurance policy, and name a trusted relative or friend or even a financial institution to be the Custodian of the gift. Should you die while the child is a minor, the insurance company will give the proceeds of the policy to the person you named as Custodian to hold until the child is an adult.

You can make a gift to a minor in your Will. You can appoint your Personal Representative (or anyone else) as Custodian of the gift. For example:

I give the sum of $20,000 to _____ (name) as custodian for _____ (name of minor) under the Florida Uniform Transfers to Minors Act.

THE LIFETIME GIFT

You can even use the Florida Uniform Transfers to Minors Law to make a gift during your lifetime of some item such as shares in a corporation or a limited partnership interest. You can nominate yourself as Custodian of the gift, or you can name another person to serve as Custodian. Once the lifetime gift is made it becomes irrevocable, so this method is not appropriate unless you are sure that you want the child to have the gift once he is an adult.

In general, the Custodian must distribute the gift when the child reaches 18; however, if you make a lifetime gift, or a gift as part of your Will, you can direct the Custodian to distribute the gift when the child reaches 21 (FS 710.104, 710.105, 710.106, 710.108, 710.123).

THE CUSTODIAN'S DUTIES

Under Florida law, while the Custodian is in possession of the gift, he can use as much of the gift as he thinks advisable for the benefit of the child. He can pay money directly to the child, or use the funds for the child's benefit.

The Custodian can do the opposite and distribute nothing. He can refuse to use any of the monies for the child and just keep the funds invested. In such case, the child's parent or guardian (or even the child once he is 14) can ask a Court to order that the monies be used for the care of the child. The Judge will determine what is in the child's best interest and then rule on the matter (FS 710.116).

Florida law requires that the Custodian keep custodial property separate and clearly identified as custodial property. He is required to keep a record of all transactions made with the property and to make those records available to the child's parent or legal guardian. If not, any member of the child's family, or the child once he/she reaches 14, can ask the Court to order a full accounting of the custodial property (FS 710.114).

As with any type of Estate Plan, you need to examine all aspects of the transfer to see if there is anything that may be objectionable to you.

THE CUSTODIAN'S FEE

The law requires the Custodian to manage the property in a responsible, prudent manner. The Custodian is entitled to be paid for his effort. If the gift is sizeable, his fee can be sizeable. Before appointing a person or a financial institution as Custodian, it is best to come to a written agreement about how the property will be managed and the charge for doing so (FS 710.114, 710.117).

NO GROUP GIFT

You cannot make a gift to more than one child under the Uniform Transfers To Minors Act. For example, you cannot make a single gift of real property to two or more minor children under the Uniform Transfers To Minors Act. If you wish to make such a gift, you would need to do so by another method, such as creating a Trust for the children (FS 710.112).

THE COST OF PROBATE

You can include a gift to a minor in your Will by naming a Custodian for the gift. But as with any gift made under a Will, a Probate procedure will be necessary to distribute the gift to the Custodian (or to the child if he is 21). If you are trying to avoid Probate, this may not be the best way to go. If your gift is significant, the better route is to set up a Revocable Living Trust. You can manage the Trust while you are able. Should you become incapacitated or die before the child is grown your Successor Trustee will take over. You can instruct the Successor Trustee to use his best discretion to either keep the funds invested until the child reaches whatever age you think proper.

Which brings us to another problem, namely, that there is no flexibility as to the final distribution of a gift made under the Uniform Transfers to Minors Act.

MANDATORY DISTRIBUTION

A Custodian appointed under the Florida Uniform Transfers To Minors Act must distribute the gift by the child's 18th birthday (21st for a gift made by Will). (FS 710.123). The gift must be made regardless of whether the child has sufficient maturity to handle the money in a responsible manner. A sizeable gift to an immature beneficiary is not the best Estate Plan.

Perhaps the reason that the story of Cinderella has such universal appeal is that many stepchildren, at one point or another, feel left out. The law seems to reinforce that perception. Unless a married person makes provision otherwise, a spouse has priority over the child in health matters both before and after death. If a married person is too ill to make medical decisions, the doctors will turn to the spouse for directions. Should a married person die, the decedent's spouse and not the child, has authority to agree to an autopsy or anatomical gift (FS 732.912).

If a married couple hold all of their property jointly, that property will go to the surviving spouse and not to the child of the deceased parent. This might not be a problem if the surviving spouse is the natural parent of the child. It could be a major problem if the natural parent dies first. The stepchild of the surviving parent may be left with nothing.

In such situations, the stepparent comes across as villain, but it is the parent, and not the stepparent, who decides whether the child will inherit property belonging to the natural parent. Too often the stepchild is left out by default, i.e., the natural parent doesn't give the matter any thought, or perhaps the natural parent is confident that the stepparent will do "what's right."

That was the case with Walter. He always wanted to be a father, so he was pleased when Todd was born just before the first anniversary of Walter's marriage to Nancy. Twin girls were born just 15 months later. Unfortunately the twins' birth was premature, causing them to have medical and developmental problems. Nancy had her hands full just caring for the three children, so it was up to Walter to support the family.

Walter was up to the job. He was both conscientious and ambitious. He started his own interior decorating business, complete with a retail sales storefront to sell fabrics, and an upholstery shop in the rear of the store. With hard work and long hours, he was able to make a comfortable living. But the strain of raising a family and running a business took its toll, both on him and the marriage. At 40, he felt like an old man.

All that changed when he hired Annie to manage the retail part of his business. Her energy and sunny disposition were just what the business (and Walter) needed.

Walter's divorce from Nancy was amicable. Walter was a loving father who took his responsibilities seriously. He was generous when it came to supporting the children. Walter had only finished high school, and he wanted more for his son. He encouraged Todd to do well in school so that he could go on to college, and maybe become a doctor or lawyer. The twins had developmental problems; but Walter encouraged them to reach their maximum potential. It was his goal to help them become self sufficient.

Annie got along very well with her stepchildren. She had no trouble with Walter's desire to support the children and give them a good start in life. Even though they held all of their money in a joint account, she never questioned any expense made on behalf of the children.

Walter never gave much thought to an Estate Plan. After all, he was healthy, and in the prime of his earning capacity. He often said that he was fortunate to have married two wonderful women. If he had a dark thought, it soon passed, rationalizing that if something happened to him, Annie would take care of the children.

But she didn't.

Walter died in one of those freak accidents. He was trimming the branches from his tree with an electric saw and accidentally touched an overhead wire. All he owned was tied up in the business that he held jointly with Annie. Annie felt that she was a major factor in the success of that business. Why should she share any of her hard earned money with Nancy? As for the children, it was Nancy's job to raise them. After all they were Nancy's children, and not Annie's children. If it was a struggle to support the children, that was Nancy's problem!

A better argument (but one she didn't raise) was that Walter really wanted Annie to inherit everything. If he wanted to provide for his children, he could have done so in any number of different ways, beginning with his marriage to Annie:

✍ He could have insisted on a prenuptial agreement that would have provided for certain funds to be kept separate for the benefit of his children.

✍ He could have signed a partnership agreement with Annie that would have given his share of the business to his children, in the event of his death.

✍ If he didn't want to negotiate with Annie about a prenuptial agreement or a partnership agreement, he could have had his attorney prepare a Trust that would have cared for the children until they were old enough to be on their own.

✍ If nothing else, he could have purchased a life insurance policy with the children as beneficiaries of the policy.

THE SECOND MARRIAGE TRUST

Walter's situation is not unique. Second marriages are commonplace in America. Many who are widowed or divorced, remarry. If children are involved, the parent may have divided loyalties. The parent may want to provide income to the child until the child completes his education and then leave whatever is left of his Estate to his surviving spouse. More often it is the other way around. The parent wants to be sure that the surviving spouse has sufficient income to support his current life style, but once the surviving spouse dies, the parent wants all that remains to go to his children. A properly drafted Trust can provide for the care of a spouse and child in whatever way the Grantor of the Trust thinks best.

That was the case with an elderly widower who married a pretty girl less than half his age. Their prenuptial agreement made it clear that all his property would go to his son from his first marriage. Surprisingly, the marriage turned out well. So well that the couple had two daughters. The husband decided to divide his Estate equally between his three children and to provide for the care of his wife until the youngest child was grown.

His attorney suggested a Trust. "You can be Trustee during your lifetime. Once you die, your Successor Trustee can immediately distribute one-third of the Trust to your son who is now 55. No sense to keep him waiting. The rest of your money can remain in your Trust. Income from the Trust can be used to support your wife and children until the youngest is 25. Then, whatever remains in the Trust can be distributed equally to your daughters."

"Good idea" said the elderly gentlemen, with a smile "Just make sure it is revocable during my lifetime. Who knows what adventures I might be up to in the future?"

It isn't just stepchildren who can be left out if no provision is made. Even children from a long-standing marriage can be cut off against the wishes of a parent. A parent may assume that all of their children will be treated equally when both parents are gone, but if all their property is held jointly, the last parent to die is the one who gets to decide "who gets what." Too often, the wishes of the deceased parent are ignored, for example:

THE STRAINED RELATIONSHIP A child may have a close relationship with one parent, and a strained, but tolerable, relationship with the other. Peace in the family is achieved because the parent who is close to the child acts as a buffer. Should the buffer parent die first, the relationship between the surviving parent and the child may fall apart altogether and the child's inheritance be cut off.

THE PARENT WITH DIMINISHED CAPACITY The more common scenario, is that the surviving parent becomes increasingly dependent on one child — either for emotional support, or for physical assistance as the parent ages. The other children may live at a distance, or perhaps they are too involved with their own family to assist. The supporting child may end up with most, if not all, of what was intended for all of the children.

These problems can be avoided by having your attorney prepare a Family Trust. The family assets are placed in the Trust with the parents as co-Trustees. The beneficiaries of the Trust cannot be changed unless both parents agree to the change. Once one parent dies, the Trust becomes irrevocable. The Trust income goes to the surviving parent and once that parent dies, whatever remains in the Trust is distributed in the manner as was agreed by both parents.

The caregiver of someone who is incapacitated, or developmentally disabled needs to, as part of his Estate Plan, provide for the care of the incapacitated person as well as himself. Should the caregiver become disabled or die, someone will need to take over and make medical decisions for the incapacitated person and see to it that he/she is properly housed and fed.

An aging parent of a developmentally disabled child may worry about how the child will manage without the parent to oversee his care. An aged spouse caring for his incapacitated spouse, may be concerned about who will care for the ill spouse should he die first. Often a family member will agree to take responsibility for the care of an incapacitated person; but perhaps no one wants the job.

If there are large sums of money involved it may be the opposite case, too many people may want to be in control. One family member may want the incapacitated child or spouse to remain at home with the assistance of a home health care worker. Another may think the best place is an assisted living facility with 24 hour care. The caregiver may be concerned that a tug-of-war will erupt once he dies.

In such case, the caregiver should consult with an attorney to ensure future care for the incapacitated person. The attorney may suggest that a guardianship be set up with the caregiver as Guardian. Once the Guardian is appointed, he can ask the Court to appoint a *Standby Guardian* to take over as Guardian should the caregiver become incapacitated or die (FS 744.304).

The only problem with setting up a guardianship while the caregiver is able to care for the disabled spouse or child is the cost of the procedure. It may cost hundreds, if not thousands, of dollars to set up and maintain the guardianship. This may not be much of a concern for the wealthy. And it is not much of a problem if the incapacitated person is without funds because the caregiver can ask Legal Aid for assistance. See page ix to find the nearest Legal Aid office.

Those who are neither rich or poor may hesitate to go through the effort and expense to set up a guardianship if it may not be needed for years to come. An alternative, is for the caregiver to make provision in his Will for the appointment of a successor caregiver. The parent of a disabled child or the spouse of an incapacitated person may use his Will to appoint a Guardian of the person or property of the incapacitated person. In fact, under Florida law, anyone who makes a gift to an incapacitated person in his Will, can name someone to serve as Guardian and the Judge will give serious consideration to that person (FS 744.312).

Once the caregiver is deceased and the Will admitted to Probate, the Guardian named in the Will can apply to be appointed as the legal Guardian of the incapacitated person. Before making the appointment the Court will need to establish that the person is in fact incapacitated and in need of a Guardian. Once that is established, the Court will determine whether your choice of Guardian is qualified; i.e., is over 18, and not a convicted felon (FS 744.309). The Judge will examine all of the circumstances of the case. If he finds that it is in the best interests of the incapacitated person to appoint the person of your choice as Guardian, he will do so.

A TRUST FOR THE DISABLED

Government assistance is available to provide medical and custodial care for those who are disabled and without the means to care for themselves. Both Florida and federal government provide such assistance with programs such as Social Security disability benefits and Medicaid. The family often supplements the government program by providing for the incapacitated person's **special needs** or **supplemental needs** such as hobbies, special education, outings to a movie or a sports event — things that give the incapacitated person some quality of life. This is not a problem while family members are alive and able to provide for the incapacitated person. The worry is how to continue that care should the provider die.

To be eligible for government assistance programs the incapacitated person must essentially be without funds. Family members fear that leaving money to the incapacitated in a Will or Trust will disqualify the incapacitated person from receiving government assistance. Parents of a disabled child may decide to solve the problem by leaving the money to a sibling or other family member with verbal instructions to take care of the child once the parent is deceased.

Of course, the problem with that approach is that once the funds are left to the family member, they become the property of the family member. As the property of the family member, they are available to his creditors. The funds could be lost in a divorce, or the family member could die and the funds inherited by someone who is not willing to care for the disabled child.

A better solution is to have an experienced Elder Law attorney set up a **Supplemental Needs Trust.** The Trust can be funded by the parent during his lifetime, or after his death by making the Trust the beneficiary of his Will or Trust. It can also be funded by a life insurance policy on the life of the parent. The parent can purchase the policy and name the Supplemental Needs Trust as the beneficiary of the insurance funds.

The Trustee of the Supplemental Needs Trust can use the monies in the Trust to provide for the child's supplemental or special needs during his lifetime. The Trust Agreement can provide that upon the death of the incapacitated person, whatever remains in the Trust be distributed to whoever the parent names as the remainder beneficiary of the Trust.

 NOT RECOMMENDED FOR DISABLED SPOUSE

The Trust we have just described is appropriate for a disabled child, who has no funds of his own. The Trust is funded with monies owned by a parent and not the child. This Trust may not be the way to go if the disabled person is married and the Trust is funded by monies owned by the well spouse. When determining eligibility, the government considers monies owned by both the husband and wife. If a Trust is set up using money owned by either of them, the government will consider the Trust funds to be available to pay for the care of the disabled spouse (42 U.S.C.1382c(a)(3), 1396p(d)(4)(A)).

In Chapter 10 we will discuss how a married couple can arrange their finances to provide for their maintenance without jeopardizing the right of the incapacitated person to qualilfy for medical assistance.

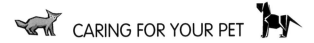 CARING FOR YOUR PET

A woman died at peace,
leaving her fortune
and care of her cat to her niece.
Alas, the fortune and the cat
disappeared soon after that.

You could leave money to someone with the understanding that the person will take care of your pet, but the moral of the above limerick, is that just leaving money will not guarantee care for your pet. The better route is to have your attorney prepare a Will that includes specific instructions and funds to provide for the care of your pet during its lifetime. Those with a Trust can include a similar provision as part of the Trust. The provision for your pet should include directions for how the remaining funds are to be distributed after the death of the pet.

A TRUST TO CARE FOR YOUR PET

If you are financially able and have several pets, you may want to set up a special Trust for the care of your pets. The person you name as Trustee will be charged with the duty to use Trust funds to pay for the care of those animals who survive you. You also need to name a residuary beneficiary (a person or perhaps a charitable organization) to receive whatever remains in the Trust once all of the animals are deceased. You can include a provision in your Trust giving your residuary beneficiary the right to a regular accounting of Trust funds; and the right to check to see that your pets are treated humanely, if not benevolently (FS 737.116).

Animal support groups, such as the Humane Society, have people who will care for the pet of a deceased owner. You might consider appointing such group as the remainder beneficiary of the Trust in exchange for the lifetime care of your pet(s).

If you don't have the resources to set up a Trust to care for your pet, you can ask you pet's veterinarian to consider starting an "Orphaned Pet Service" to assist in finding new homes for pets who lose their owners. It is good public relations and a potential source of income. If this is agreeable to the Veterinarian, you can make arrangements in your Will to pay the Vet to care for the pet until a suitable family can be found. This is a more humane approach than the, all too common practice, of putting a pet "to sleep" rather than have the pet suffer the loss of its master. And in at least one case, that reasoning backfired.

Eleanor always had a pet in the house. After her husband died, her two poodles were her constant companions. When Eleanor became ill with cancer, she worried about what would happen to her "buddies" without her to care for them. She finally decided it best to have her family put them to sleep when she died. Eleanor endured surgery, chemotherapy, radiation therapy, and even some holistic remedies, but she continued to go downhill. Eleanor's family came in to visit her at the hospital to say their last good-byes. She was so ill, she didn't even recognize them. No one thought she could last the day. Because the family was from out of state, and time short, they decided to put the pets to sleep so they need only take care of the funeral arrangements when she died.

To everyone's surprise, Eleanor rallied. She lived two more long, lonely years. She often said she wished they had put her to sleep instead of her buddies.

THE CHARITABLE TRUST

We explained how a Trust can be set up to care for a pet and whatever is left over (the remainder) given to a charitable organization. There are other kinds of charitable trusts that can be set up to benefit the giver as well as the receiver. For example, suppose you own stock which has appreciated substantially over the years, but pays few dividends. This hasn't been a problem in the past because you earned a good income. But now you wish to retire, and will need additional income. You would like to cash in the stock and invest the funds in something that can supplement your retirement income, but your accountant says that a significant portion of the value of the stock will go to Uncle Sam as payment for the Capital Gains Tax.

By now you know that a clever Estate Planning attorney will have any number of ways to solve the problem. The dialogue with your attorney might go something like this:

ATTORNEY: "Do you have a favorite charity?"

"Yes, why do you ask?"

ATTORNEY: "You can set up a Charitable Remainder Trust and donate the stock to that charity by depositing the stock in the Trust. Charities don't pay taxes, so the stock can be sold and the proceeds invested in property that produces a good income. In return for the donation, you can receive an income for the next 20 years or you can receive a monthly annuity based on your life expectancy."

"What's in it for the charity?"

ATTORNEY: "The charity gets whatever is left after paying you the annuity."

"Yes, but suppose I die next year, and my wife is left without the securities and no income."

ATTORNEY: "No problem. If you decide on a 20 year annuity, you can name your wife or any other beneficiary to receive the balance of the annuity. If you wish, you can have an annuity based on your life expectancy and that of your spouse. If you predecease your spouse, then the income continues until she dies."

"It seems to me that if the annuity is based on my life expectancy AND my wife's life expectancy, there won't be much left for the charity."

ATTORNEY: "How much is left for the charity depends on the value of the gift and the cost of the annuity. The cost of the annuity depends on the combined life expectancy of you and your wife. I think the best way to understand this plan is for you to look at actual numbers. There are any number of ways to set up a Charitable Remainder Trust. I can explain each option to you. For each option, I will give you the cost of setting up the program; the amount of money you will get; and how much money will actually go to your favorite charity. Of course, it must be an IRS approved charity. Once you see the numbers you can make an informed decision as to whether you want to sell the stock and pay the Capital Gains Tax, or set up a Charitable Trust and receive an income."

"Good idea."

THE FUTURE OF ESTATE PLANNING

Up till now Estate Planning for the wealthy was all about the Estate Tax. Estate Planning attorneys would spend their time dreaming up different ways to reduce Estate taxes for their wealthy clients. The IRS would spend their time examining and challenging any Estate plan that appeared too innovative. It seems likely that by 2010 the Estate Tax will be a memory. Is the game over?

Hardly. As explained in Chapter 3, instead of paying an Estate Tax, the child who inherits property that has appreciated more than 1.3 million dollars will pay a substantial Capital Gains Tax when he sells the property. In a way, that makes sense. A major criticism of the Estate Tax was that the tax had to be paid within 9 months of the date of death. That created a hardship for those inheriting a small business with a high assessed value but with no cash to pay taxes on that value.

Critics of the Estate Tax often cited the example of the cash poor farm located on valuable land. Once the owner of the farm died, the family would be forced to sell the farm just to pay Estate Taxes. By substituting the Capital Gains tax for the Estate Tax, that problem is eliminated. No Capital Gains Tax need be paid until the beneficiary decides to sell the property. Theoretically, the family farm can now be inherited generation to generation with no tax consequence.

But there are few family farms in today's economy. Future heirs are more likely to inherit highly appreciated real property or securities that they will eventually want to sell. And when they do, they may need to pay a significant Capital Gains Tax.

The new game for Estate Planning attorneys will be to devise an Estate Plan that will reduce the Capital Gains Tax. The IRS will, no doubt, enjoy challenging those plans.

One tried (and legal) method of reducing the Capital Gains Tax is the Charitable Remainder Trust as was just discussed. It doesn't take a crystal ball to see that this could well be the basis of future Estate Plans, so we will take a few more pages to describe the pros and cons of the Trust.

THE CHARITABLE REMAINDER ANNUITY TRUST

A ***Charitable Remainder Annuity Trust*** is a Trust that is established according to the Internal Revenue Code (IRC 664). Charities do not pay taxes, so property donated to the Trust can be sold by the Trustee free of the Capital Gains Tax. Money from the sale is invested so that it provides an income (an *annuity*) to the beneficiary (the *annuitant*) for a fixed period of time, say 20 years, or for the annuitant's lifetime as computed by actuarial tables (i.e., life expectancy tables). The charity receives whatever is left (the *remainder*) after payment of the annuity. How much income the donor will receive and how much the charity will receive, is agreed upon at the time the Trust is set up.

The Trust can be set up in any number of ways depending on the goal of the ***donor*** (the person making the gift). In the example just given, the goal of the donor was to convert non-income producing property to income producing property without paying a high Capital Gains Tax. A wealthy donor may be more concerned about his child paying a high Capital Gains Tax should the child inherit highly appreciated property.

For example, suppose you bought acreage in Northern Florida that appreciated significantly over the years and is now worth 1 million dollars. You have been putting off selling the property because of the Capital Gains Tax. But it has been a burden to you. It produces no income and because the property continues to appreciate, each year you are paying more and more in property taxes. You did not mind the sacrifice because you figured that your son would inherit the property at a step-up in basis. But now with the new tax law, by the time you die, the property may be worth 2 million dollars. He is only allowed a 1.3 million dollar step up in basis, so your son may need to pay a significant Capital Gains Tax when he sells the property.

Setting up a Charitable Remainder Annuity Trust solves the problem of the Capital Gains Tax. The land is transferred to the Charitable Trust. Charities pay no tax, so the Trustee can sell the land and the full market value of the property will be available for investment.

The Trust could be set up with you receiving an income for life, and your son receiving the annuity after your death. The only problem with this arrangement is that your son is significantly younger than you are. There may not be much left to benefit the charity if they must wait for both of you to die. The solution is to have the annuity based on your life only and then use part of the income that you receive to purchase a two million dollar insurance policy on your life with your son as beneficiary. The two million dollars is the estimated value of the land that your son would have inherited at your death. But with this arrangement he will inherit the insurance proceeds free of any Capital Gains Tax.

The astute reader (and probably one with an accounting background) will say "Aha, you may have avoided the Capital Gains Tax, but the Estate Tax Exclusion value does not increase to 2 million dollars until the year 2006. The 2 million dollar life insurance policy counts as part of your taxable Estate, so if you die before 2006, your son will pay an Estate Tax! "

And of course our clever imaginary attorney has a solution in the form of an Irrevocable Insurance Trust. You can set up an Irrevocable Trust so that the Trust owns the insurance policy and not you. The insurance policy is not included in your taxable Estate, so your son pays no Estate Tax. See the end of Chapter 6 for an explanation of how the Irrevocable Insurance Trust works.

As with any Estate Plan, you need to consider the down-side, and the Charitable Remainder Annuity Trust is no exception.

⊠ ATTORNEY FEES

It may cost significant attorney fees to set up the Trust. Some charities may offer to have their attorney prepare the Trust at no cost to you, or perhaps they offer a "standard" Trust document that their attorney prepared. But, using their Trust document represents a conflict of interest. Their Trust was prepared by an attorney for the greatest benefit to his client (that's the charity, not you). It is important that you employ your own attorney to represent you. He knows the extent of your Estate and he understands what you wish to accomplish.

⊠   THE COMPLEXITY OF THE PLAN

A Charitable Remainder Annuity Trust is a sophisticated Estate Plan designed to benefit the well-to-do donor and an IRS approved charity. There are any number of ways to set up the plan. It is important to have an attorney who will take the time to explore different plans until you determine the best plan for you.

⊠   THE TRUST IS IRREVOCABLE

Once established, the Trust is not revocable, so it is important that you understand all of the aspects of the Trust. In particular, you need to know how much it will cost in attorney's fees to set up the Trust; and how much income you will receive, and over what period of time. The income you receive as an annuitant is taxable to you. You need to consider that while taxes change over the years, the terms of the Trust cannot be changed. It is important that your attorney, accountant or financial planner give you some idea of what you might expect in terms of future income tax payments.

Although future income tax payments may be a question mark, the power of the Charitable Remainder Trust is the tax benefit to the donor at the time the Trust is set up.

☑   NO CAPITAL GAINS TAX

Had you sold the property and invested the money yourself, you would have paid a Capital Gains Tax and that tax could have been substantial, depending on the tax rate in effect at the time of the transfer. By gifting the property the full value of the land can be used to produce investment income.

☑   NO PROPERTY TAX

Once your property is transferred into the Trust, you will no longer need to pay annual property taxes.

☑   NO GIFT TAX

The property you transfer into the Trust is a gift to a charity and as such is not included in the sum total of taxable gifts that you give during your lifetime.

☑   INCOME TAX DEDUCTION

Because you are making a charitable donation, you should be able to take a charitable deduction on your income tax in the year of the donation.

There are other "perks" in addition to the tax benefits:

☑   NO PROBATE EXPENSE

It might take an expensive and time consuming Probate procedure to transfer the property to a beneficiary upon your death. By transferring the property to the Trust during your lifetime, you avoid the need for a Probate procedure to transfer the property after your death.

☑   GIVE WHEN NEEDED INSTEAD OF LATER

A Charitable Remainder Annuity Trust can be set up in any number of different ways to accommodate your Estate Plan. For example, if you are not in need of a present income, but expect that you will spend significant sums on your child's education, you can set up a 20 year annuity with your child as the annuitant. This will get the child through college and probably be a great help should the child decide to start a family. Why have the child inherit property in later, high earning years rather than in the early, high expense/low income years?

☑ CREDITOR PROTECTION

If you keep the land and are sued, you could lose it to pay your creditors. If a beneficiary inherits the land, it could be lost to his/her creditors. But once the property is transferred to the Trust, the gift is made. Neither your creditors nor your beneficiary's creditors can gain access to the Trust funds. The most a creditor can do is seek payment from the money that is received as an income.

☑ GOOD DEED

If you are concerned that your son will be tagged with a Capital Gains Tax once you die, it means that your property has appreciated more than 1.3 million dollars, and you are fortunate indeed. By setting up a Charitable Trust, you are making a donation to the charity of your choice. You are sharing your good fortune with others. You can consider this as "giving back" to the community, or just plain doing a good deed.

BECOME A PHILANTHROPIST

Instead of giving the property to an established charity, you can become a philanthropist and set up your own Charitable foundation. The foundation can be in the form of an IRS approved Charitable Trust. You can be the Trustee of the Charitable Trust and your child the Successor Trustee. The Trust can be set up according to your specific charitable purposes. You can use the Trust to benefit a single cause or several worthy projects. This can be an exciting adventure for those with ample resources and a community spirit.

An Estate Plan For Your Person

The law makes a distinction between your property (what you own) and your person (your body). We have been discussing how to set up an Estate Plan for your property with the goal of maximum control over your Estate during your lifetime, and minimum cost and hassle to your heirs once you die. An Estate Plan for your body is just as important as an Estate Plan for your property. The goals are much the same. Maximum control over your body during your lifetime. Minimum cost and hassle to your family for your final disposition.

You may think it strange to speak of planning for maximum control of your body during your lifetime. After all, it's your body. Who else but you has any right to control what you do with your body? That may be true so long as you have capacity, but should you become seriously ill, you may be unable to express your wishes about the care you wish to receive. If you do not have an Estate Plan in place for your person, then your next of kin, or maybe the state of Florida may make health decisions for you.

The same applies to the final disposition of your body. If you don't make Preneed burial and/or funeral arrangements, then someone will need to make those decisions for you.

As this chapter will show, it is relatively simple and inexpensive to set up an Estate Plan for your Person.

MAKING BURIAL ARRANGEMENTS

People with a large family often arrange for a family burial site. Over the years deceased family members come to occupy a space in that site, but others may have been buried elsewhere. Surviving family members often lose track of the number of spaces left. If this is the case with your family, then you need to take inventory of the number of spaces available and who in the family expects to use those spaces.

It is important to keep in touch with the cemetery and let them know whenever you move and/or when there is a change in the identity of the intended occupant. Florida law requires that an owner of a burial site keep the cemetery informed, in writing, of their current address. If, after 50 years, the cemetery is unable to locate the owner of the burial site, it will consider the burial site to be abandoned. The site will not be considered abandoned if there are two or more adjoining sites owned by someone, and at least one of those common sites is currently occupied (FS 497.353).

OUT OF STATE BURIAL SITE

It may be that the family burial site is not in the state of Florida. In such case, it is important to consider the cost of transporting the body from Florida to the out-of-state cemetery. That cost can be substantial, in some cases doubling the cost of the burial. If there is no emotional attachment to the out-of-state burial site, you may want to consider assigning the burial site to a family member who lives closer to the site and making your own burial arrangements here in Florida.

It is important to make your own burial arrangements. Even if it is not important to you where you are buried, it may be very important to your family. That is often the case in second marriages. If you have children from a first marriage, they may want their parents to be "reunited in death." Your current spouse may not take kindly to having you buried with your former spouse. This might result in hard feelings, if not an out-and-out battle.

The same problem can arise with those in a gay relationship. The decedent's family might not have acknowledged the relationship. The family might decide to have the decedent buried in the family plot and exclude the gay partner from participating in the burial arrangements.

You can head off disputes about your final resting place, by making your own burial arrangements. If you do not do so, then the person with authority to decide the matter for you is determined by Florida statute.

Under Florida law, the person with priority to decide your final disposition is as follows:

1st	spouse
2nd	a child who is 18 or older
3rd	a parent
4th	a grandchild who is 18 or older
5th	a grandparent
6th	any next of kin (FS 470.002 (18)).

Florida Courts have ruled that the surviving spouse has top priority, even if the couple were separated prior to the death (*Andrews, et al. v. McGowan*, et al. Fla App. 5 Dist. No 98-2883, 1999).

Increasingly people are opting for cremation. The reasons for choosing cremation are varied, but for the majority, it is a matter of finances. The cost of cremation is approximately one-sixth that of an ordinary funeral and burial. A major saving is the cost of the casket. A casket is not necessary for the cremation. An alternate container of fiberboard or similar materials, can be used to transport the body. Embalming is not necessary either, unless there is to be a funeral with a viewing. Federal law prohibits a funeral director from saying that a casket or embalming is necessary for a direct (immediate) cremation (16 Code of Federal Regulations ("CFR") 453.3 (b)(1)(ii)).

For those who are considering cremation, there are a few things to consider.

THE PACEMAKER

Cremating a body with a pacemaker or any radiation producing device can cause damage to the cremation chamber and/or to the person performing the cremation. If you have such an electronic aid, it will need to be removed prior to the cremation. You might check with the cremation service to determine the cost of having the pacemaker removed.

A pacemaker can be donated for use in animals with a medical need for the service. If you are interested in making such donation, you can ask your local veterinarian to refer you to an animal clinic that performs the procedure, and then arrange to have it removed prior to your burial or cremation.

THE OVERWEIGHT

Cremation may not be an option for those who weigh more than 300 pounds. Many cremation services do not have the facilities to handle a large body. If you weigh more than 300 pounds, you need to check with your local cremation service to determine whether this will be a problem.

WHAT TO DO WITH THE ASHES

In addition to planning for the procedure, you need to give your family some guidance as to where to place the ashes. Some cemeteries allow an urn containing the cremated remains of a family member to be placed in an occupied family plot. Similarly, some cemeteries will allow the cremated remains to be placed in the space in a mausoleum that is currently occupied by a member of the decedent's family. If you intend to be cremated and all your family spaces are occupied you may want to call the cemetery and ask them to explain their policy as it relates to the burial of urns in occupied sites.

If burial in the family site is not an option, you will need to arrange for a separate burial space. Many cemeteries have a separate building called a *columbarium*, which is especially designed to store urns. You can purchase a storage place for the urn in the same manner as the purchase of a burial space in a cemetery.

If you wish to have your cremated remains scattered, you need to let your next of kin know where and how this is to be done. If you want your ashes spread out to sea, your family will need to arrange to have a boat go out at least three nautical miles, because federal law prohibits ashes from being scattered any closer than that distance from land (Title 40 CFR Section 229.1).

THE MILITARY BURIAL

If you are an honorably discharged veteran or the spouse of such veteran, you have the right to be buried in a Veterans National Cemetery. If your Veteran spouse was buried in a Veterans National Cemetery then you have the right to be buried in that same grave site unless soil conditions require a separate grave site.

You can get information about burial at a Veterans National Cemetery by calling the Veteran's Administration at (800) 827-1000, or visiting their Web site.

 VA CEMETERY WEB SITE
http://www.cem.va.gov

The site has information on the following topics:
 - ➤ National and Military Cemeteries
 - ➤ Burial, Headstones and Markers
 - ➤ State Cemetery Grants Program

You cannot reserve a grave site in advance, so your family will need to make arrangements and establish your eligibility to be buried in a Veterans National Cemetery. At that time, they will need to provide the following information:
 - ➤ your rank, serial, social security and
   VA claim numbers
 - ➤ the branch of service in which you served;
   the date and place of your entry into and
   separation from the service
 - ➤ a copy of your official military discharge
   document bearing an official seal
   or a DD 214 form.

If you wish to be buried in a national cemetery, you need to make all of these items readily accessible to your family.

If you are financially able, in addition to arranging a burial space, consider purchasing a Preneed Funeral Plan. It will be easier on your family emotionally and financially if you make your own funeral arrangements.

Federal law requires that you receive a general price list at the beginning of any discussion for the purchase of funeral services (16 CFR 453.2). Once you decide upon a plan, the seller should give you a contract that states the prices charged for *services* (embalming, viewing, transportation, etc.) and *merchandise purchased* (casket, urn, acknowledgment cards, register books, flowers, clothing, etc.) and *cash advance items*; i.e. things paid for by the funeral director and then reimbursed back to him. This includes paying for death certificates, having the obituary printed, paying for religious services, etc. (16 CFR 453.5, FS 470.002, 497.333).

In addition to federal law, Florida regulation requires that the seller use a form approved by the Florida Board of Funeral and Cemetery Services (FS 497.101, 497.409). Even though the seller gives you a form approved by the Board, it does not mean that it cannot be changed. If you are not satisfied with the way a certain section of the contract reads, then attach an addendum to the contract that explains, in plain English, your understanding of that passage. If you are concerned about something that is not mentioned in the contract, insist that the contract be amended to include that item.

In particular, check to see whether the contract answers the following questions:

Does the contract cover all costs?

The contract should contain an itemized list stating exactly what goods and services are included in the sales price. Your contract may include an allowance towards cash advance items such as the printing of the obituary or payment to the clergy, or your contract may provide that payment be made at the time of the funeral. Your contract should state that the amount charged by the funeral director for a cash advance item be no more than the amount paid by the director for that item.

Is the price guaranteed?

Some Preneed Funeral plans have a fixed price for the goods and services you choose, meaning that the funeral director will provide the goods and services at the same price as agreed at the time of the contract. It is important that your contract state that the person or company who is selling you the Funeral Plan is the same person or company who will actually provide those goods and services. If not, you need to have the provider of the goods and services sign the contract saying that he agrees to be bound by the terms of your agreement. If the seller says that it is not necessary for the provider to sign your contract because he and the provider have a separate written agreement, have that agreement attached to your contract.

You might opt for a Preneed Funeral Contract that is not a fixed price; meaning that the company can charge additional monies for the plan that you have chosen upon your death. In these days of an ever increasing life expectancy, it is important that such a contract clearly state how the price will be determined when the contract is finally put into effect.

How are your contract funds protected?

You may decide to pay cash for your Preneed Funeral Plan. In that case, Florida law requires that the funds be protected. There are different ways to do so under Florida law.

THE SELLER'S TRUST

The seller can deposit the funds into a Trust according to Florida statute 497.417. The amount deposited depends on what you purchased. The seller must deposit 70% of the monies paid for services; 100% for cash advance items; 30% of the purchase price or 110% of the wholesale price (whichever is greater) of the casket and other items of merchandise sold. The buyer has no control over this Trust. It is considered to be a Seller's Trust. The seller may ask the Board to be allowed to post a bond payable to the Board instead of placing the funds into a Trust. If the company is large enough, the Board may allow the company to provide a Letter of Credit in place of the bond (FS 497.423, 497.425).

THE BUYER'S TRUST

The contract can provide that the funds be placed into a Trust according to Florida statute 497.429. In this case the seller has no control over the Trust. It is considered to be a Buyer's Trust. If the buyer is purchasing the Preneed Plan on an installment basis, the buyer will deposit the funds directly into the Trust. This gives the buyer greater protection however, there are downsides. Any interest earned on the Trust is taxed to the buyer each year as income, but when the contract is performed or cancelled, all of the interest goes to the seller. If the buyer cancels the contract within the first 3 years, the seller is entitled to keep 10% of the Trust funds. The contract should say how much of the funds can be kept by the seller if the buyer or his heirs decide to cancel the contract after the first 3 years.

SERVICE FEE

With both the Seller's and Buyer's Trust, the Trust Company may charge a service fee to manage the account. The Trustee may charge an initial service fee and an annual service fee as a percentage of the interest earned on that account. Your contract will probably state that you will forfeit the initial and annual service fee should you decide to cancel your contract.

If you are paying cash for the plan, it is important that your contract clearly explain how your Trust funds are going to be protected; i.e., with a Seller's Trust (or bond or Letter of Credit) or with a Buyer's Trust. Have your contract state exactly how much will be charged as a service fee.

THE CONSUMER PROTECTION TRUST FUND

For each contract sold, the seller of a Preneed Funeral contract is required to deposit a nominal sum ($2.50 up to $10, depending on the contract value and plan) into a Consumer Protection Trust Fund that is regulated by Florida Board of Funeral and Cemetery Services. The purpose of the Protection Trust Fund is to reimburse buyers of a Preneed Plan in the event that the company does not deliver the goods and services paid for by the buyer (FS 497.413).

This is not to give the buyer a false sense of security. Many local funeral homes are owned by a large parent organization. If the parent organization has given the Board a Letter of Credit instead of a bond, then it could happen that the company goes into bankruptcy and the Consumer Protection Trust Fund would not be adequate to protect 100% of the monies paid by consumers.

Can you cancel the contract?

Florida law gives you the right to cancel your Preneed Funeral Contract within 30 days of signing the agreement and to receive all of your monies back. After 30 days the amount you will receive back depends on the terms of the contract. If you are purchasing a Preneed Funeral contract on an installment plan and you are 90 days late in making payment, the seller can cancel your contract and keep all of the money you paid. However, under Florida law, if you give the seller 30 days notice that you are exercising your option under Florida statute 497.419, he must refund any money you paid for services or cash advance items.

It is important that your contract clearly indicates your right to cancel the contract and what amount you will receive should you cancel the contract.

FUNERAL PLANS FOR THOSE ON PUBLIC ASSISTANCE

People who are applying for Medicaid, Supplemental Security Income ("SSI") or other public assistance program have limits on the amount of assets that they own. Monies paid into a Preneed Funeral Plan count as an asset because the purchaser of the plan can cancel his contract and get his money back. Understanding the problem, the Florida legislators included a provision in the law allowing those who are applying for SSI, Medicaid, or Temporary Cash Assistance, to make their plan irrevocable, so it will not count as an asset (FS 497.419).

Even if you are in good health at this time, it is a good idea to have your contract provide that you can make your plan irrevocable, if at any time you need to apply for a public assistance program.

Is the funeral firm reputable?

It is important to take the time to check up on whoever is selling you the contract. In Florida, anyone who offers Preneed Funeral contracts to the public must be licensed to do so. You can check to see if the seller is licensed by calling the Florida Comptroller's Office (800) 323-2627. You may also want to ask how long they have been in business and whether any complaints have been filed against them.

Suppose you die in another state or country?

Your contract should spell out what provision will be made in the event that you move to another state or die in another state or country. Many funeral firms are part of a national funeral service corporation with funeral firms located throughout the United States. You may be able to have the contract provide that there will be no additional charge if the contract is performed by one of the funeral firms owned by the parent company.

Can the plan be changed after your death?

It may happen that your heirs need to cancel your Funeral Plan after your death because:

➤ your body is missing or cannot be recovered, or

➤ you were buried by another facility because no one knew that you had a Preneed Funeral Contract, or

➤ you died in another country and were buried there.

Your contract should address these potential problems, and spell out how much money will be refunded and who is to receive the refund. You may also want to specify whether your heirs have the right to alter your funeral plans. In the absence of such a provision in the contract, funeral firms usually allow the family to arrange for a more expensive plan, provided they agree to pay the difference.

You may wonder why anyone would think of changing the decedent's funeral plan, but consider that in today's market, it is not uncommon for a Preneed Funeral Plan to cost several thousand dollars. A top end funeral complete with solid bronze casket can cost upwards of $30,000. Some heirs might be motivated to save money by changing the plan to one of a lesser value.

That was the case with Lester. His mother, Mona, was a difficult woman with a personality that can only be described as "sour." Her husband deserted her after four years of marriage leaving her to raise Lester by herself. Once Lester was grown, Mona made it clear to him that she had done her job and now he was on his own. Lester could have used some help. He married and had three children. One of his children suffered with asthma and it was a constant struggle to keep up with the medical bills.

Mona believed in being good to herself. She did not intend to, nor did she, leave much money when she died. She knew that Lester would not be able to afford a "proper" burial for her, so she purchased a funeral plan and paid close to $18,000 for it. She was pleased when the funeral director told her that the monies would be kept safely in a Trust account until the time they were needed.

Lester was not familiar with Florida law, so when his mother died he asked an attorney at the Legal Aid office to determine whether the Preneed Funeral contract could be cancelled and a lesser priced funeral arrangement be made — maybe cremation.

It was.

You know the ending to this story.

The reader might be thinking "Revocable. Irrevocable. All this contract stuff is giving me a headache. Why can't I just set aside some money and let my kids figure it out?"

The problem with that approach is that the cost of your final illness may leave you with little or no funds for your burial. To avoid the problem, you could purchase a life insurance policy to fund your funeral and burial, naming one or two trusted family members as the beneficiary of the policy. It is important that the person who is to receive the insurance funds clearly understands why he/she is named as beneficiary of the policy. It is equally important that the beneficiary agree to use the monies for the intended purpose.

It isn't so much that a family member is not trustworthy as it is that they may not understand what you intended — especially in those cases where other funds are available to pay for the funeral. Too often insurance funds are left to a child who refuses to contribute to the cost of the funeral saying "Dad wanted me to have this money. That's why he left it to me."

To avoid a misunderstanding, put it in writing. It need not be a formal contract. It could be something as simple as a letter to the insurance beneficiary, with copies to your next of kin. See the next page for an example of such letter.

> *Dear Paul,*
>
> *I purchased a $20,000 insurance policy today naming you as beneficiary of the policy.*
> *As we discussed this money is to be used to pay for the following:*
> *- my funeral; grave site and headstone*
> *- perpetual care for my grave*
> *- airfare for each of my grandchildren to attend the funeral*
> *- dinner for the family after the wake*
> *- lunch for the family after the funeral*
>
> *If there is any money left over, please accept it as my thanks for all the effort spent on my behalf.*
> *Love,*
> *Dad*
>
> *P.S. I am sending a copy of this letter to your sister so that she will know that all arrangements have been made.*

Whether or not you arrange to pay for your burial or funeral, you need to let your next of kin know your feelings about the burial procedure. Let your family know whether you wish to be cremated or buried. If you wish to have a religious service, then let your family know the type of service and where it is to be held. Let the family know where you wish to be buried, or if you intend to be cremated, then where to place the ashes.

ANATOMICAL GIFT

Those who wish to make an anatomical gift upon their death can include the gift as part of their Will; but it may be some time before the Will is located. The better route is to make the donation by a separate writing. If you wish to make an anatomical gift, you can complete an **ORGAN AND TISSUE DONOR CARD** when you apply for your Florida driver's license or Florida Photo Identification Card. The Florida Department of Highway Safety and Motor Vehicles will include your gift in a registry that is accessible to hospitals on a 24 hour basis (FS 765.515, 765.521).

If you do not want the fact that you are an organ donor indicated on your driver's licence or Photo ID, you can sign a Donor Card and give it to a trusted family member. Florida statute (FS 765.514) contains a **UNIFORM DONOR CARD** that you can complete to make the donation. You can download the donor card from the Florida statute Web site.

FLORIDA STATUTE
http://www.leg.state.fl.us

You can also appoint a **HEALTH CARE SURROGATE** and give him authority to make the donation on your behalf. We will discuss how to appoint a Health Care Surrogate later in this chapter.

GIFT FOR EDUCATION AND RESEARCH

There is no age limit on organ and tissue donations, however doctors will probably not consider your body suitable for transplantation if you are of advanced age and in poor health. You can still donate your body to a school of medicine or dentistry for education and research. The ANATOMICAL BOARD OF THE STATE OF FLORIDA coordinates the donation program for the state of Florida. The Board distributes the gift to the closest school. You can preregister by calling them at (800) 628-2594, or you can write to them for information.

THE ANATOMICAL BOARD OF THE STATE OF FLORIDA
University of Florida, Health Science Center
P.O. Box 100235
Gainsville, FL 32610-20235

There is an embalming fee and a transportation charge to deliver the body to the school. If you make such a gift, then give your family instructions about what to do in the event that you die far from home.

If you do not wish to make an anatomical gift, then let your family know how you feel. Florida law also prohibits a gift if the decedent ever expressed an objection to making an anatomical gift. If you do not make provision for a gift, and do not tell anyone how you feel, the decision will be up to your family. Florida statute (FS 765.512) gives an order of priority for those who can give permission to make an anatomical gift:

1st	spouse	2nd	adult son or daughter
3rd	either parent	4th	adult brother or sister
5th	a grandparent		
6th	the Guardian of the decedent at time of death.		

No gift can be made if someone agrees to the gift and someone with higher priority objects; and an anatomical gift cannot be made by the spouse if any of the decedent's adult children object.

AUTOPSIES

An autopsy is one of those things that most of us do not think about; reasoning that if it is needed, it will be carried out and, being dead, you will have no choice in the matter. But there are many times when an autopsy is optional. Sometimes a doctor is not sure of the cause of death, and asks the family to allow an autopsy. It is often in the family's best interest to consent to the autopsy. The examination might reveal a genetic disorder, that could be treated if it later appears in another family member. Death from a car "accident" could have been a heart attack at the wheel. Perhaps the patient who died suddenly in a hospital was misdiagnosed. The nursing home resident could have died from negligence and not old age. Even if none of these are found, knowing the cause of death with certainty is better than not knowing.

If you appoint a HEALTH CARE SURROGATE (someone to make your medical decisions), then he can agree to the autopsy. If you do not appoint a Surrogate, your spouse or nearest relative may consent to the procedure (FS 872.04 (2)).

The person giving authorization for an optional autopsy must agree to pay for the autopsy because the cost is not covered under most health insurance plans. An autopsy can cost anywhere from several hundred to several thousand dollars. Still another reason family members hesitate to allow the procedure is that they do not know how the decedent would have felt about the examination.

If you have strong feelings one way or another, then it is important to let your family know whether you would want an optional autopsy.

Of course, there are problems with just telling someone how you feel about your burial arrangements, autopsies, and anatomical gifts:

YOU TELL THE WRONG PERSON

You may tell someone who does not have authority to carry out your wishes. That was the case with James. When his wife died, he moved to a retirement community where he lived for several years until his death. James had two sons who lived in different states. Although he loved his sons, he had difficulty talking to either of them about serious matters. It was easier for him to talk with his friends in the retirement community. They often spoke about dying and how they felt about different burial arrangements. James would reminisce about his youth and growing up in a farming community in the plains state of Kansas. "I was happy and free. Out there you had room to breathe. It would be nice to be buried there — peaceful and spacious."

When he died, his friends told his sons about their father's desire to be buried in Kansas. They met the suggestion with scepticism and pragmatism:

"Dad didn't say anything like that to me."

"It would cost us double, if we had to arrange for burial in another state. I'm sure he didn't have that kind of expense in mind."

THE PERSON DOES NOT CARRY OUT YOUR WISHES

Sometimes the person you tell about the disposition of your body may not understand what you said or perhaps they hear only what they want to hear. Whether they follow your burial instructions or authorize an autopsy or anatomical gift may depend more about what costs are involved, and their own feelings, rather than what you may have wanted.

Even if you tell someone and trust that person to carry out your wishes, it could be that the person you confide in cannot carry out your instructions. For example, if you tell your spouse what arrangements to make, he/she may become incapacitated or die before you do; or perhaps you both die together in a natural disaster or in a plane crash.

WHO WANTS TO TALK ABOUT IT?

For many people the main problem with telling someone what to do when you die is talking about your death. It may be an uncomfortable, if not unpleasant, subject for you to bring up, and for your family to discuss. If this is the case, then consider putting the information in writing and give the instructions to the person who will have the job of carrying out your wishes.

Making provision for the disposition of your body is important, but it is more important to make sure that you are in control of the health care you receive should you become seriously ill. This is not a problem when you are well enough to make your own medical decisions; however it could happen that you are too ill to let people know what you want.

You can appoint a Surrogate to carry out your wishes relating to your health care, by signing a document entitled *Designation of Health Care Surrogate.* Florida statute (FS 765.203) contains a statutory form that you can copy from your nearest law library or you can download it from the Internet. http:// www. leg.state.fl.us.

The statutory form gives your Health Care Surrogate authority to make your medical decisions in the event you are unable to make them yourself. If there is any question about whether you are capable of making your own health care decisions, your physician will evaluate your condition. If he determines you do not have capacity to make decisions, he will put the evaluation in writing and deliver it to your Health Care Surrogate. Your Surrogate will then be responsible to give consent for your treatment (FS 765.204).

USING THE DESIGNATION FOR FINAL DISPOSITION

The statutory form of Designation of Health Care Surrogate has an optional ADDITIONAL INSTRUCTION section. You can use that section to allow your Surrogate to make an anatomical gift of your body, or to authorize an autopsy if necessary (FS 872.04). If you have not made Preneed Funeral arrangements, then it is a important to include directions for your final disposition in that section. By doing so, your Health Care Surrogate will have authority to carry out your instructions. If you made Preneed Funeral arrangements, then give a copy of your contract to your Health Care Surrogate.

If the disposition of your final remains is important to you, then it is important that you give your Health Care Surrogate authority to carry out your instructions. If you neglect to do so, then the family member with authority to dispose of your remains is as explained on page 154.

Even if you do not have strong feelings about your final disposition, it is important to give a single person authority, else two people with the same priority might disagree. That was the case with the remains of Ted Williams. His son and daughter had a lengthy, and no doubt expensive, court battle over whether the remains of the famous baseball player should be cremated or preserved in a frozen state.

Many of us have little concern that anyone would go to Court over the disposition of our remains, yet there could be a family spat over the issue. Best to take the time to appoint a Health Care Surrogate and eliminate the potential for such disagreement.

THE LIVING WILL

In addition to appointing a Surrogate, it is important that you let your Surrogate know whether you do (or do not) want life support systems to be used in the event that you are dying and there is no hope for your recovery. You can tell your Surrogate how you feel, but the better route is to sign a *Living Will*. Florida Statute (FS 765.303) has a suggested form for the Living Will. You can copy that document from the law library or you can download it from the Florida Statute Web site.

The statutory form of Living Will allows you to appoint a Surrogate to carry out the directions given in your Living Will. You can appoint the same person you chose in your Designation of Health Care Surrogate; or you can appoint someone different in your Living Will to determine whether life support systems should be discontinued. Choosing two different people might lead to some confusion, so it is better to choose the same person to make all of your medical decisions, and an alternate in case your first choice is not available.

MEDICAL DECISIONS IF NO HEALTH CARE SURROGATE

If you do not appoint someone to make your medical decisions in the event you are too ill to do so yourself, then the State of Florida does so for you by giving the following people priority to make medical decisions:

1st   a court appointed Guardian (if any)

2nd   the patient's spouse

3rd   adult child; or if more than one child a majority of the children available for consultation

4th   the patient's parent

5th   an adult brother or sister; or a majority of those siblings available for consultation

6th   an adult relative who has exhibited special care and maintained regular contact with you

7th   a close friend (FS 765.401).

A person with priority must be reasonably available, willing and competent to make medical decisions for you. If not, the next one with priority will make the decision.

If the above order of priority is not as you wish, or if there is someone you wish to exclude altogether from making your health care decisions, then it is important to appoint the person of your choice to act as your Health Care Surrogate. If not, life decisions made for you, may not be as you would have wished.

George is a case in point. His wife suffered from Alzheimer's disease. He cared for her at home for as long as he was able, but finally, it was too much for him and he placed her in a local nursing facility. He and his two daughters visited her frequently, even though she scarcely recognized them.

George met Emily during one of his visits. Her husband also suffered from Alzheimer's and was a resident of the nursing home. George and Emily had much in common. After visiting with their respective spouses, they would go to the local coffee shop. One thing led to another and soon they were an item.

George's daughters were not happy with his "lady friend." They criticized everything about her. From the way she dressed, to her table manners. Emily did not take it personally. She believed the girls were more interested in their expected inheritance than George's happiness. A second marriage might cut into what they considered to be rightfully theirs.

Not that George and Emily planned to wed. They both loved their respective spouses and had no intention of trying to obtain a divorce. They just enjoyed each other's company. Caring for their respective spouses, they learned to take it one day at a time. That philosophy carried over into their relationship. They were both content to enjoy social outings with each other — dinner, movies, playing golf, and so on.

Both were happier than they had been in years. But that happiness was short-lived. George suffered a stroke while driving a car. He was seriously injured and lapsed into a coma. The prognosis was not encouraging. The doctors said George would die unless they put him on a ventilator and inserted a feeding tube. Even with life support systems, they were not promising that he would survive.

Emily pleaded to keep him alive. "Let's try everything. If he doesn't improve, we can always discontinue the life support systems later."

George's daughters did not see it that way. "Why torture him with needles and tubes. Let him pass on peacefully."

George never signed a Living Will, so no one knew how he felt about life support systems. He never appointed anyone to be his Health Care Surrogate to make his medical decisions now that he was unable to do so himself. In the absence of a Designation of Health Care Surrogate, the doctors followed Florida law. George's spouse had priority to direct his treatment however because she was unable to do so, his daughters had the right to make medical decisions for their father.

Emily being 7th in priority had no legal authority to direct his treatment.

George died.

A Health Care Estate Plan 9

We discussed an Estate Plan as it relates to the distribution or management of your Estate once you are deceased. In this age of extended life expectancy, a more pressing concern is how to manage and preserve your Estate in the event of a debilitating illness. As life expectancy increases, so does the percentage of the population who suffer incapacitating strokes, Alzheimer's disease or Parkinsons' disease. It is estimated that more than half of the population who are 85 or older, have some degree of dementia. Your best Estate Plan could be sabotaged by a lengthy illness. In this chapter we explore ways to pay for the health care you may require as you age.

In addition to paying for your health care, you need to consider who will care for your finances and everyday physical needs in the event that you are too ill to do so yourself. A *Health Care Estate Plan* is a plan designed to care for your person and property in the event of an incapacitating illness. In the last chapter, we discussed how you can appoint a Health Care Surrogate to care for your person in the event of your incapacity.

But there is still the problem of who will care for your property. In this chapter we will discuss how you can appoint someone to care for your property and manage your finances in the event of your incapacity.

The optimum way to provide for the care of your property in the event of your incapacity is to set up a Trust appointing a Successor Trustee to care for your property according to the directions given in your Trust. You can be Trustee of the funds while you have capacity. Should you become incapacitated, then the person you name as Successor Trustee will take over. But if you do not have sufficient assets to justify the cost of employing an attorney to draft a Trust, then there are other strategies that you can use to solve the problem.

THE JOINT ACCOUNT

You can set up a joint checking account so that a trusted family member can write checks on the account. Of course there are all the inherent problems of a joint account that we discussed in Chapter 2. You can avoid many of those problems by limiting the amount of money that can be accessed by the family member. For example, you can arrange your finances so that all of your bills are paid from a single checking account and your family member can access that account, only.

THE CONVENIENCE ACCOUNT

If you set up a joint account, your family member will own whatever is in the account should your die. If this is not as you wish, you can instruct the bank that this is a *Convenience Account* and that in the event of your death the family member may no longer access your account. But ultimately the family member must be trustworthy because the bank is under no duty to stop your family member from writing checks on your account until the bank learns of your death (FS 655.80).

The Joint Account and the Convenience Account solve the problem of how to pay your bills in the event you are temporarily ill. It does not solve the problem of how to manage your business affairs in the event of an extended illness. For example, suppose you have a stroke and can no longer be cared for at home. Should it be necessary for you to sell your home and move to an assisted living facility, no one will have the authority to sell the house for you. In such case, the Court will need to appoint a Guardian to manage your finances, and if you did not appoint a Health Care Surrogate, to make your health care decisions as well.

Setting up the guardianship is time consuming and expensive. Whoever believes you are unable to manage your person or property, can petition the Court to determine whether you need a Guardian. The Court will appoint a three member Examining Committee at least one of whom is a psychiatrist or physician. After the examination, a competency hearing will be held. You can have your own attorney represent you at the hearing. If you do not have an attorney, the Court will appoint one for you (FS 744.331).

If it is determined that you are incapacitated, there will be a hearing to decide who will serve as your Guardian. Your attorney can represent you at that hearing as well. The Court may decide to appoint a Guardian of your person or property, or both. If a Guardian of your property is appointed he will take possession of your assets and file an inventory with the Court. The Court may order your Guardian to obtain a bond for the protection of your assets (FS 744.351, 744.361).

Each year the Guardian must account to the Court for monies spent. Your Guardian may need to employ an accountant to help prepare the inventory and annual accounting. If a Guardian of your person is appointed, he will see to your health care. He will need to prepare and file a report each year regarding your well-being (FS 744.367, 744.3678).

The Guardian is entitled to be paid reasonable compensation for his services. Florida statute 744.108 lists several items to be considered by the Court when setting the fee, including:

⇨ the time and labor required to serve as Guardian

⇨ the fee usually charged in the area for serving as a Guardian

⇨ the value of the property of the incapacitated person

⇨ the relationship of the Guardian to the incapacitated person

⇨ the experience, reputation, diligence and ability of the Guardian

The fees for the Guardian's attorney must be approved by the Court. The rate paid to the attorney is comparable to fees paid to the attorney of other fiduciaries such as a Trustee or Personal Representative.

Court filing fees, the competency examination fee, the cost of a bond, accounting fees, the Guardian's fee, your attorney's fee and the Guardian's attorney fees, all are paid from your Estate (that's your money!).

Guardianship procedures are expensive to set up and maintain. Curious that so many people worry about how to avoid Probate, when the greater concern should be how to avoid guardianship. Consider that it is not all that hard to arrange your finances so that no Probate is necessary. The cost to transfer your property to your beneficiaries should be minimal.

Even with a full Probate procedure, whatever it costs to Probate your Estate is a one-time expense. And Probate is a one-time procedure. Once monies are distributed to your beneficiaries, it is over. Not so if you become incapacitated. It can cost thousands of dollars to set up the Guardianship; and more money to care for you and your property each year. And this expense goes on, year after year, until you are returned to capacity, or die (FS 744.521).

As with Probate it is not all that hard to avoid these unnecessary charges to your Estate. To avoid the need for a Guardian of your person, you can appoint a Health Care Surrogate to make your medical decisions should you be too ill to do so yourself (see Chapter 8).

To avoid the need for a Guardian of your property, you can set up a Trust and appoint a Successor Trustee to care for your property in the event of your incapacity. For those of limited means, the **DURABLE POWER OF ATTORNEY** is the next best Estate plan.

A Power of Attorney is a legal document by which someone (the **Principal**) gives another (his **Agent** or **Attorney-In-Fact**) authority to do certain acts on behalf of the Principal. If you wish to have someone to conduct business on your behalf in the event you become physically incapacitated, you can make the Power of Attorney **durable** by including the phrase "This durable power of attorney is not affected by the subsequent incapacity of the principal except as provided in s. 709.08." Florida statute 709.08 provides that a Durable Power of Attorney remains in effect unless the Principal dies or revokes the Power of Attorney. It is also not effective in the event a Court determines that you are legally incapacitated. In such case the Court will appoint a Guardian to take over the management of your finances.

GENERAL POWERS

You can draft your Durable Power of Attorney so that your Agent has broad general powers to manage your finances and do much the same with your property as you can do yourself. You may include the power to:

⇨ buy or sell real property on your behalf;

⇨ buy or sell personal property for you;

⇨ trade in securities (stocks, bonds, etc.)

⇨ pay your bills and/or taxes;

⇨ operate your business;

⇨ have access to your safe deposit box;

⇨ borrow money on your behalf;

⇨ purchase insurance policies and name beneficiaries;

⇨ sue or defend a law suit on your behalf;

⇨ apply for government benefits on your behalf;

⇨ have access to your business and personal records.

You can even give your Agent power to make gifts of your property in accordance with your Estate Plan, for example, you can direct him to give certain family members up to $11,000 in gifts each year.

Notice that there are many things that your Agent can do for you personally, such as defending a law suit or suing on your behalf, or applying for government benefits. Even if you have a Trust, it is important to appoint an Agent under a Durable Power of Attorney to do these important, personal, things for you, in the event you can't. Your Trust can only authorize your Successor Trustee to manage property that is placed in your Trust. Your Successor Trustee has no authority over you, personally. But you can give him (or anyone else) that authority by making him your Agent under a Power of Attorney.

GENERAL VS. LIMITED POWER OF ATTORNEY

You can sign a Power of Attorney giving your Agent broad general powers. With these powers your Agent can do much the same with your property as you can. Instead of a General Power of Attorney, you can limit the things your Agent can do with your property to just those things that you authorize in your Power of Attorney. One power that should be specifically granted in your Power of Attorney, is the power to apply for medical assistance benefits in the event of your incapacity. In the next chapter we will be discussing the many things you can do to qualify for Medicaid. You need to give someone authority to take the necessary steps for you to become eligible for government benefits, in the event you are too ill to do so yourself. Even if you do not wish to give someone control over your finances at this time, you should give someone a Limited Power of Attorney for the purpose of qualifying for Medicaid.

Limited or General, the operative word in any Power of Attorney is POWER. Once your Agent has authority to act, he essentially steps in your shoes and can do whatever you gave him authority to do. Your primary consideration in choosing an Agent is trustworthiness. You need to choose someone who will follow your instructions and put the Power of Attorney to the use you intended. You need to choose someone, who, when using your Power of Attorney, will always put your interests ahead of his.

You may be less concerned with trustworthiness than the loss of independence. But the thing to keep in mind is that you still have the power to do all of the things you gave your Agent authority to do. The only difference is that now, you both have the power to conduct your business transactions.

Of course, shared authority is still less independent than sole authority; so you may hesitate to give someone a Power of Attorney until it is needed. But if you wait until you need it, you may be too sick to sign the document. There are two solutions to the dilemma. One is to keep the document in your possession.

USING THE POWER OF ATTORNEY

An Agent under a Power of Attorney cannot operate on behalf of the Principal, unless the Agent has possession of the original Power of Attorney and presents it to whomever he wants to rely on that document. For example, if your Agent wants to use the Power of Attorney to sell one of your securities, he will need to produce the original document and perhaps sign an Affidavit (a written statement sworn to before a Notary Public) saying that the Power of Attorney is still in effect and that you did not revoke that Power of Attorney.

KEEP THE DOCUMENT IN YOUR POSSESSION

Before anyone (a bank, stockbroker, closing agent, etc.) will accept the Power of Attorney they will want to see the original document so that they are assured that your Attorney-In-Fact has authority to transact business on your behalf. If you keep the original document in your possession and do not give anyone a copy, your Attorney-In-Fact will not be able to act for you.

The only problem with this arrangement is that you need to arrange to make the document accessible to your Agent in the event of your incapacity. If your Agent is a trusted family member, you can give him the location of the document with instructions to take possession of the Durable Power of Attorney in the event of your incapacity.

THE SPRINGING POWER OF ATTORNEY

A better solution may be to have your attorney draft a "springing" Durable Power of Attorney that is not operational until your family doctor and/or independent physician says that you are incapacitated and unable to manage your financial affairs.

Your Agent can hold the original document, but cannot use it until it "springs to life" when a doctor determines that you are too ill to care for your property. You can create a Springing Durable Power of Attorney by adding the following provision to the document

> This Durable Power of Attorney becomes operational only when my regularly attending physician and _____ (name of family member) sign an Affidavit stating that I am disabled or incapacitated.

USING THE POWER OF ATTORNEY FOR MEDICAL DECISIONS

Your attorney can design a Durable Power of Attorney, to meet your special needs. He can even include powers that relate to your health care. But as a practical matter, it may be better to have a separate Health Care Advance Directive. As explained in the previous chapter, the Health Care Advance Directive can be used to appoint a Health Care Surrogate and to give your Surrogate directions about the care you wish to receive in the event you are too ill to direct your medical treatment. There are two reasons to have a separate Health Care Advance Directive:

APPOINT DIFFERENT PEOPLE TO SERVE

You may want one person to serve as your Health Care Surrogate and another to serve as your Agent. One family member may be an excellent choice to make your health care decisions, yet that person may not be the best person to make financial decisions on your behalf.

PRIVACY

Even if you want the same person to serve as your Health Care Surrogate and Agent under a Power of Attorney, there is still the matter of privacy. Your Health Care Surrogate will give a copy of your Health Care Advance Directive to your physician to be placed in your medical file. Your doctors have no need to know of your business dealings; and vice versa. To conduct business on your behalf your Agent will need to give a copy of the Power of Attorney to your business associates (banks, stockbrokers, etc.). Your business associates have no need to know of your medical decisions.

For privacy, and perhaps security reasons, consider using separate documents, rather than try to get it all into a single multi-purpose document.

It is relatively simple and inexpensive to head off guardianship. All you need do is appoint an Agent under a Durable Power of Attorney to manage your finances and a Health Care Surrogate under a Designation of Health Care Surrogate to make your medical care decisions. These documents authorize people of your choice to care for you and your property in the event of your incapacity.

But, despite your best plans, something unusual could happen causing a Court to decide that you or your property needs protection. For example, you might develop an addiction or a mental illness causing self-destructive behavior. Your friends or family might decide that you are in need of protection and ask a Court to appoint a Guardian to care for you.

Although it may not be possible to avoid all guardianship procedures, you can have a measure of control over your fate. Florida statute gives you the right to name the person of your choice to serve as your Guardian (FS 744.3045). You can do this by appointing a **Preneed Guardian**. This is done in much the same manner as appointing a Preneed Guardian for a minor child as was explained in the last chapter.

APPOINTING A PRENEED GUARDIAN

You can sign a declaration appointing someone to serve as your Guardian in the event a Court determines that you are incapacitated. You will need to sign the Declaration in the presence of two witnesses; and then file the Declaration with the Clerk of the Circuit Court in the county of your residence.

Should you ever be declared to be incapacitated, your Preneed Guardian can immediately take over the job of Guardian. Within 20 days, your Preneed Guardian must ask the Court to be appointed as your legal Guardian. The Court will do so, unless there is some legal reason not to, such as a Preneed Guardian who is under 18, or a convicted felon, or who is unable to serve because of his own incapacity or illness (FS 744.309).

Many readers will wonder if it is really necessary to go through all this. After all what is the probability that you will ever be determined to be incapacitated? If ever you are incapacitated, what is the probability that there will be a Court battle over who should serve as your Guardian? And what is the probability that the person appointed by the Court would not be your choice of Guardian?

These probabilities are small for a young, single person, with loving parents. They are also small for a married person with a caring spouse. But take the case of a single person with a serious addiction who is estranged from his family; or a single, elderly person with several children or relatives, all who would want to serve as Guardian; and these probabilities increase significantly.

Married or single, if you are in the process of setting up your Estate Plan, or changing your existing plan, consider having your attorney prepare and record a Declaration appointing the person of your choice to serve as your Preneed Guardian, should the need ever arise. If circumstances change over the years, you can always revoke the Declaration and appoint another to serve as your Preneed Guardian.

The good news is: You are going to live longer.
The bad news is: It's going to cost you.

Scientists are doing a great job of prolonging life, but unless they find Ponce De Leon's fountain, the general population will age. Along with age comes infirmities. Eyes fail. Hearing diminishes. Mobility declines. Digestive systems either speed up or slow down, all to the discomfort of the unhappy occupant of the body. It's all part of the "golden" years.

The pharmacology industry is well motivated to produce drugs that manage the ills associated with aging. Their research has led to a wealth of pharmaceutic products that do not cure, but do allow people to live in relative comfort into advanced age. The only problem is the cost of these drugs. Medicare covers the treatment of life-threatening brushes with heart disease, stroke, cancer and diabetes; but, as of this writing, Medicare does not pay for maintenance medication that is often necessary once the condition is stabilized.

Medicare is also limited in long term care coverage. It does not pay for extended nursing care. Medicare pays for the first 20 days of skilled nursing care. You pay up to $105** per day for days 21 through 100. If you do not have Medicare Supplemental Insurance coverage, it will cost you up to $8,400 for the next 80 days. After 100 days, you are on your own. A nursing home stay of one or two years can wipe out the life savings of most working people. Once savings are gone, the government provides care in the form of Medicaid coverage.

**This is the value for the year 2004. The federal government adjusts the amount each year.

If you have no assets to speak of, and an income beneath the poverty level, then the cost of long-term nursing care is the least of your worries. Medicaid is available to take care of your medical and nursing care needs. And no need to worry if you are wealthy. You have enough money to pay for any care that you might need. The rest of us need to think about ways to provide for long-term health care.

For those concerned about the loss of life savings because of illness, there is supplemental and/or long-term health care insurance. There are many different insurance plans available. You can call the National Association of Insurance Commissioners at (816) 842-3600 and they will forward to you, free of charge, the publication:

A SHOPPER'S GUIDE TO LONG TERM CARE INSURANCE

If you have a specific question, you can call the Florida **DEPARTMENT OF ELDER AFFAIRS** for a referral to one of their trained Information Specialists or you can visit their Web site for information.

 FLORIDA DEPARTMENT OF ELDER AFFAIRS
http://elderaffairs.state.fl.us/

LONG TERM INSURANCE FOR FEDERAL EMPLOYEES

The Long Term Care Security Act (Public Law 106-265) was passed by Congress to take effect in October, 2002. The law is designed to make long term care insurance available to federal and postal employees, members of the uniformed services, civilian and military retirees, and their qualified relatives. You can call the Office of Personnel Management at (800) 582-3337 for information about the program or visit their Web site.

 OFFICE OF PERSONNEL MANAGEMENT
http://www.opm.gov/insure/ltc

The National Association Of Retired Federal Employees ("NARFE") has been actively involved in developing this legislation. You can get information about the program at the NARFE office in Alexandria, Virginia at (703) 838-7780 or from their Web site.

 NATIONAL ASSOC. OF RETIRED FEDERAL EMPLOYEES
http://www.narfe.org

THE PROBLEM OF COST AND ELIGIBILITY

Long term care insurance sounds like the perfect solution, until you start examining the cost. The cost isn't too bad if you are comparatively young, say in your 50s. But can you imagine paying that premium each month until you are in your 80s and never needing nursing care?

Many decide to wait till they are old and going downhill. But that just brings other problems. The older you are, the greater the cost of insurance. And there is the risk that you will be refused coverage because of a "pre-existing" condition, i.e., the insurance company may consider you to be too great a risk for them to insure.

Different insurance companies have come up with insurance plans that may provide a solution for the person who is relatively young and in good health. Some companies offer long-term care insurance that is paid-up within a fixed period of time. Once payments are made for a certain number of years, the person is insured for long-term care without further payment. Other companies combine long-term care insurance with a life insurance policy. They offer long-term care insurance that converts to a life insurance policy, if it happens that the insured person dies before needing long-term care. When shopping for a long-term care policy, consider including different insurance alternatives in your investigation.

For some people long term care insurance is not an option. An elderly person living on a low fixed income may not have enough money to pay the monthly premium for a long term care insurance policy. And long term care insurance is not an option for the person who has been diagnosed with a chronic, debilitating disease.

People in such a position worry that they may need to deplete their life savings, just to pay for a year or two of nursing care.

Both of these problems can be solved by using current law to become qualified for Medicaid. Medicaid is a public assistance program that is funded jointly by the federal and state government. There are state and federal laws governing who may become eligible for the program.

A *Medicaid Qualifying Plan* is a plan that takes both state and federal laws into consideration. Operating within the boundaries of these laws, those who are concerned about becoming impoverished in order to pay for long-term care, seek to preserve and protect their Estate by implementing a Medicaid Qualifying Plan.

There has been controversy about plans designed to qualify a person for Medicaid. Some think that to intentionally arrange finances to qualify for Medicaid is immoral — a legal method of working the system.

Those people may argue: "Why are such things allowed? After all, wasn't Medicaid designed to help poor people? Why should people be allowed to make themselves poor to get on the public dole??

Those who feel they need to qualify for Medicaid have a different point of view. They may argue:

"I worked all my life and hoped to leave a few pennies for the kids. Why did I work so hard? To give it all to a nursing home? I paid my taxes just like everyone else. The government pays hundreds of thousands of dollars for people on Medicare to have open heart surgery, and they pay for lengthy and expensive cancer treatments. Why should those who have Alzheimer's or Parkinsons or those who suffer a debilitating stroke, not be entitled to receive equal benefits?"

Although we can understand and appreciate both points of view, our job, as we see it, is to just explain the law as it is at the time of publication. We think it is important to do so because many people take a position (pro or con) based on what they perceive the law to be, and not based upon the law as it actually is.

Once the reader understands what it takes to qualify for Medicaid in the state of Florida, he can decide for himself whether the law is basically fair to the people who need to qualify, or whether it is flawed (either too restrictive or too liberal) and needs to be changed.

Hopefully, those with a strong opinion will share those views with their legislators.

A Medicaid Qualifying Plan 10

A better name for this chapter might be "A Health Care Contingency Plan." A lengthy stay in a nursing home is something most of us do not want to even think about, much less prepare for. Why prepare for something that may never happen? Yet as we age, there is that nagging "What if?" "What if I need long term nursing care? How will I pay for it?"

An effective way to put this anxiety at rest is to have a contingency plan. To form a contingency plan, you need to know your options. In this case, your options are directly related to your ability to pay for that care. But it is hard to predict future fortunes. People win the lottery. Those with a large portfolio may have their fortunes disappear in a market melt-down. There is no need for concern if it turns out that you can afford to pay for your own nursing care; and there is no concern should you become impoverished because there are government programs that provide for your health care. The worst case scenario is that you will be able to afford long-term care, but at the cost of your life savings.

In this chapter, we will discuss options available to you under that worst case scenario. We will explain current state and federal law as it relates to qualifying for medical assistance programs.

Once you know the law, you will be able to form a contingency health care plan that is right for you.

WHO IS ENTITLED TO MEDICAID?

Medicaid is a program that provides medical and long term nursing care for people with low income and limited Resources. The program is funded and regulated by both federal and state government. The governing agency for the federal government is the Centers for Medicare and Medicaid Services. In Florida, the Agency for Health Care Administration is the state agency with authority to make payments for medical assistance programs including Medicaid. Applications are taken and the program administered at the local level by the Department of Children and Family Services (FS 409.902).

Medicaid is an entitlement program, meaning that whoever qualifies for the program is entitled to receive benefits under that program. Those who do not qualify are not entitled to any Medicaid benefits.

There are many benefits offered under Medicaid, from health care for mothers and children; to community based services for those who need some assistance with their health care; to full nursing care for those who need assistance with dressing, bathing, eating, walking and toileting. We will limit our discussion of Medicaid to aged persons in need of institutional nursing care. You can get information about other Medicaid programs by calling your local Department of Children and Family Services. You can also get information about Medicaid from the Health and Human Services section of the Agency For Health Care Administration Web site.

 FLORIDA HEALTH AND HUMAN SERVICES
http://www.fdhc.state.fl.us

Persons who are receiving Supplemental Security Income ("SSI") may be automatically eligible for Medicaid because the requirements for these programs are much the same. A person who is not receiving SSI, may be eligible for Medicaid if he is 65 or older, or blind, or disabled (FS 409.904, Florida Administrative Code "FAC" 65A-7.111).

When a person applies for Medicaid (the "Applicant"**) at the Department of Children and Family Services, an *Economic Self-Sufficiency Specialist* ("ESS") will investigate his citizenship, medical condition, income, and assets. If the Applicant is too ill to apply for himself, his spouse or a responsible family member may apply for him (FS 409.901, The ESS Program Policy Manual "ESS Manual" 1040.0107).

CITIZENSHIP ELIGIBILITY
To be eligible for Medicaid, the Applicant must be a resident of the United States, and either a U.S. citizen or a non-citizen who has lawful immigration status (ESS Manual 1440.0102).

MEDICAL ELIGIBILITY
The Applicant needs to be evaluated to determine whether he has a mental or physical condition that requires 24 hour observation with constant availability of medical and nursing care (FAC 59G-4.180). If the Applicant is not currently a resident of a nursing facility the ESS may do a Pre-admission screening to determine whether the Applicant qualifies medically for the Medicaid institutional care program.

** For simplicity, we will use the male gender for the Applicant and the female gender for his spouse.

In Florida, there is a limit on the amount of income earned by the Applicant each month. For the year 2004, the Applicant may have no more than $1,692 as a monthly income. If the Applicant is over this *Income Cap* by even one penny, he will be disqualified. However, this problem is easily solved, because the state of Florida allows the excess income to be place in a *Qualified Income Trust*. A Qualified Income Trust is a Trust drafted according to state and federal law. Each month the Applicant's excess income is added to the Trust. The Trust must be irrevocable with the state of Florida as the beneficiary of the Trust. Once the Applicant dies, the Trust property is used to reimburse the state for monies spent on his behalf (FAC 65A-1.713).

An experienced Elder Law attorney can draft the Trust in conformity with state and federal law. Once drafted the Applicant can immediately qualify for Medicaid — provided, of course, that he meets all other medical and asset limit criteria.

The reader may be wondering why the state of Florida has an Income Cap when it is so easily overcome. The monies placed in a Qualified Income Trust eventually go to the state. Why not (as other states do) simply require the Applicant to contribute all of his income towards the cost of his nursing care? This is one of those questions to ask your legislator.

PERSONAL NEEDS ALLOWANCE

Once the Applicant is approved and becomes a recipient of Medicaid benefits, i.e. a *Medicaid Recipient,* he is allowed to keep a certain amount of his income each month (currently $35) for his personal needs, such as clothing or hair cuts (FAC 65A-1.714).

In addition to the Income Cap, there is a limit on the amount of **Resources** owned by the Applicant. Resources are assets owned by the Applicant, either by himself or together with another, that are countable for purposes of qualifying for Medicaid. The Applicant may have no more than $2,000 in countable Resources, unless his income is less than $683 per month; and in that case he is allowed to keep up to $5,000. An Applicant who is over the Resource limit on the first day of the month that he applies for Medicaid needs to "spend down." If he is eligible at any time during the month that he applies, his Medicaid benefits will begin on the first date of that month (FAC 65A-1.712, 1.716).

If the Applicant is married, there are limits to his spouse's Resources as well. If his spouse lives in their home in the community (i.e., not in a nursing home) she is referred to as the **Community Spouse**. Prior to 1988, the Community Spouse was required to use whatever assets she had to pay for the nursing care of her spouse. The Applicant could not quality for Medicaid until they both were virtually impoverished. In addition to being unfair to the Community Spouse, this was not good government policy because it often resulted in the impoverished spouse turning to local government social service programs for support. The Medicaid provisions of the Medicare Catastrophic Coverage Act of 1988 remedied the situation by considering the assets of the couple as being part of a common pot and allowing the Community Spouse to keep up to $92,760 of their combined Resources. The federal government also considers that the Spouse needs income each month for her maintenance. If her income is not sufficient to support her, the income of the Medicaid Recipient can be used to supplement the income of the Community Spouse up to a maximum of $2,319 per month.

The federal government adjusts these values annually for cost of living increases. The values quoted are those used in 2004 (42 U.S.C. 1382b). Notice that $2,319 for monthly income and $92,760 for Resources are the maximum values set by the federal government. States have the right to administer the Medicaid program according to their state law, provided their state law is within federal guidelines and does not exceed the maximum values set by the federal government. This being the case, the actual amount allowed to the Community spouse can vary significantly state to state.

THE SPOUSE'S INCOME

The current value set by the state of Florida as the Community Spouse's *Minimum Monthly Maintenance Income Allowance* is $1,562. The ESS considers $469 of this value to be used for shelter (condo maintenance fees, mortgage, rent, property taxes, etc.). If the spouse's shelter costs are greater than $469, the spouse is allowed an *excess shelter allowance*, provided the total value allowed as her monthly Income Allowance does not exceed the federal value of $2,319 (ESS Manual 2640.0119.03).

If the Community Spouse has an income that is greater than the amount determined by ESS as her monthly Income Allowance, then none of the Recipient's income is available to her. If her income is less than the monthly Income Allowance, then the Recipient's income can be used to supplement her income. For example, if her monthly income is $2,000 and ESS finds that she needs the full $2,319 each month, she is allowed to keep $319 of the Recipient's income each month. If for some reason (high medical bills, the need for special care, etc.) she needs more than $2,319 a month, she can appeal to have that value increased. See the next chapter for a discussion of the appeal process.

Assets owned by the Applicant or his spouse, are considered to be available to the Applicant for purposes of Medicaid eligibility. Under federal law, the Community Spouse is entitled to keep a share of the couple's assets up to the current maximum of $92,760. That share is called the *Community Spouse Resource Allowance* (42 U.S.C. 1396r-5(c)(2), 1396r-5f).

The Applicant is allowed to keep $2,000. This means that between them, a married couple could keep a total of $94,760. But suppose the couple has $200,000 worth of assets between them. In such case, they are over the Resource limit by $105,240.

The first question to ask in such a situation is whether all of their assets count as a Resource.

What Counts As A Resource?

Property owned by the Applicant, or his spouse, that can be converted to cash and used for their support, are considered to be a Resource. This includes bank accounts, certificates of deposit, property in a Revocable Living Trust, stocks, bonds, and so on (ESS Manual 1640.0501, 1640.0566, 1640.0576.07).

Some items owned by the Applicant, or his spouse, can be converted to cash, but are not counted as a Resource. These items are called "Non-Countable Resources" or "Excluded Assets." We will refer to them as EXCLUDED RESOURCES (42 U.S.C. 1382b).

RESOURCES THAT DO NOT COUNT

The following items are *Excluded Resources* and do not counted as a Resource for purposes of Medicaid Eligibility.

HOUSEHOLD GOODS AND PERSONAL EFFECTS

⇨ Any item needed because of a person's medical or physical condition is an Excluded Resource. This includes wheelchairs, special hospital beds, computers with special screens for the visually impaired, etc.

⇨ An engagement ring and/or a wedding ring do not count as a Resource, regardless of its value.

In general, clothing, jewelry, tools of a trade, pets, household goods such as furniture and appliances do not count as a Resource. However, if the Applicant lists a household item or some personal item as being worth more than $500 on his application form, ESS may decide to investigate further. If they find that the market value of the Applicant's personal property exceeds $2,000, they will count anything over $2,000 as a Resource (ESS Manual 1640.0563, 1640.0565.01, 1640.0565.03, 1640.0565.04).

LIFE INSURANCE

⇨ A life insurance policy owned by the Applicant, or his spouse, is an Excluded Resource, provided the face value (the amount paid at death) is $2,500 or less. If the face value is greater than $2,500, the Cash Surrender Value of the policy is counted as a Resource.

The exclusion value of $2,500 applies to each individual separately. If there is more than one policy on the same person, and the sum of their face values is greater than $2,500, then the Cash Surrender Value of those policies count as a Resource (ESS Manual 1640.0554, FAC 65A-1.712).

BURIAL ARRANGEMENTS

⇨ Burial spaces for the Applicant and his immediate family members (spouse, child, step-child, parent, sibling and the spouse of these family members) are Excluded Resources. Prepaid burial space items such as caskets, headstones, opening and closing of the grave, are also Excluded Resources (ESS Manual 1640.0515, 1640.0516).

⇨ An Irrevocable Preneed Funeral Plan as described in Chapter 8 is an Excluded Resource. If the Applicant or his spouse has a revocable Preneed Funeral Agreement, ESS will allow him to make that plan irrevocable so that it will qualify as an Exempt Resource (ESS Manual 1640.0509, 1640.0510).

⇨ The Applicant may set aside up to $2,500 for burial expenses. The burial fund is an Excluded Resource provided it is placed in a separate account and identified as a burial fund for the Applicant. The burial fund is available as an Excluded Resource even if there is an insurance policy on the Applicant's life of up to $2,500 and even if the Applicant has an Irrevocable Preneed Funeral Plan of $2,500 or more. The Community Spouse may also set up a separate burial fund of up to $2,500 as an Excluded Resource (ESS Manual 1640.0514).

ONE AUTOMOBILE

⇨ One automobile, regardless of its value or use is an Excluded Resource. Any other automobile counts as a Resource, with the exception of cars that are modified to accommodate a handicapped person.

To evaluate non-exempt automobiles, ESS uses the average trade-in value less any loans on the car. They do not count cars over 7 years old unless it is a luxury car (Cadillac, Mercedes, Jaguar, Corvette, etc.) or an antique vehicle (ESS Manual 1640.0591, FAC 65A-1.712(2)(e)).

THE HOME

⇨ Property owned by the Applicant as his homestead either in his name only, or together with another, is an Excluded Resource. This includes mobile homes, condominiums, cooperative apartments, and even houseboats (ESS Manual 1640.0534).

The Applicant's home is an Exempt Resource so long as it is his primary residence or that of his dependent relative. If the Applicant is in a nursing home, and no family member lives in the home, it remains an Excluded Resource, provided the Applicant, or the person who applied on his behalf, indicated that the Applicant intends to return home (ESS Manual 1640.0543.01).

RETIREMENT FUNDS

⇨ Retirement funds that are being paid periodically to the Applicant or his spouse, count as income and not as a Resource. However, if the Applicant or his spouse has a pension plan (including IRA or Keogh Plans), and is not receiving a regular payout, then the cash value of the retirement fund counts as a Resource. ESS will deduct early withdrawal penalties from the cash value of the retirement fund, but they will not subtract taxes due for an early withdrawal (ESS Manual 1640.0505.04, 1640.0505.05).

INCOME PRODUCING PROPERTY

⇨ Property that produces income to the Applicant (or his spouse) is an Excluded Resource provided it produces a reasonable rate of return and such income is essential to his support. Income-producing property includes business equipment (computers, copiers, etc.), farm animals and livestock, special tools, work vehicles (trucks, tractors, etc.), rental property (vacation cottages, condominiums, etc.).

Promissory notes and mortgages owned by the Applicant are income producing property so they do not count as a Resource, however, the income from the loans count as income to the Applicant (ESS Manual 1640.0548, FAC 65A-1.712).

PROPERTY THAT IS NOT SALEABLE

⇨ Property owned by the Applicant or his spouse must be readily able to be converted to cash in order to count as a Resource. A Life Estate interest in real property, shares held in a close corporation with no current market value, certain irrevocable annuities, and other non-saleable items can be considered as Excluded Resources.

Real property owned jointly by the Applicant and another counts as a Resource unless the Applicant is unable to sell the property without the consent of the joint owner and the joint owner refuses to sell (ESS Manual 1640.0305.02, FAC 65A-1.712).

A Will is Not Enough in Florida

JOINTLY OWNED ASSETS

The ESS considers the full value of a jointly owned bank account to be available to the Applicant, or his spouse; unless it can be proven that the other owner contributed toward the property. For example, if the Applicant owns a joint account with his son, the entire balance counts as a Resource unless the son can prove that he contributed his own money to that account. The son's net contribution (how much he contributed less how much he withdrew) does not count as a Resource (ESS Manual 1640.0302.01).

OTHER EXCLUDED RESOURCES

We listed many of the more common items that the ESS considers to be Excluded Resources. But this is not a complete list. There are other items that the ESS will not count as part of the Applicant's Resources. An experienced Elder Law Attorney will be able to examine all of the property owned by Applicant and tell him what assets ESS considers to be Excluded Resources.

Now that we know what does (and does not) count as a Resource, the next question is what options are available to our couple who are over the Resource limit by $105,240. Those with no knowledge of the law, might think the only option available to this couple is to pay for his nursing care until the $105,240 runs out. Those who carefully read the previous pages, might suggest that the couple check to see whether they can use the money to purchase items that do not count as a Resource.

THE SPEND-DOWN OPTION

Both state and federal law allow the Applicant and his spouse to use their excess Resources to purchase Excludable Resources, without losing the right to receive Medicaid benefits, provided they pay a fair market value for the item. This being the case, the couple can make funeral or burial arrangements if they have not already done so, including setting up a burial fund bank account of $2,500 for each of them.

They can purchase household items such as furniture, a television set, a new refrigerator or stove, etc. (ESS Manual 1640.0609.04).

REPAIRING EXEMPT ITEMS

Paying money to repair exempt items is a good spend-down strategy. Perhaps the exempt family car needs new brakes, or tires. The Community Spouse may decide to replace the exempt car with a new model.

If the house is in need of repair or improvement, then this is the time to fix it up. A new heating, plumbing or electrical system can use up funds quickly.

If the couple do not own their own home, the Community Spouse might consider using the excess cash as a down-payment on a home.

Some sceptics might think $105,240 is a lot of money to spend down. Maybe the couple previously made all funeral arrangements. Perhaps they really don't need (or want) new furniture or appliances. In such case, the solution may be to pay off all of their outstanding debts. If the couple has a credit card balance, they can reduce the balance to $0. If their car is an Excluded Resource, then they can pay off any money they may owe on the car.

Paying off loans is a valid spend-down strategy because it is just a return of monies given to the Applicant by the lender for the purchase of an Excluded Resource (home, car, clothing, household items). The Applicant will need to prove to the ESS, that the monies he spent were used to pay off a valid debt. If he paid off a credit card debt, the ESS will want to see the original contract with the company and the monthly bill showing what items were purchased. If a car loan was paid, the ESS will want to see the original promissory note (marked "PAID"), as well as other loan items, such as a chattel mortgage.

If the money was used to pay down a mortgage on his home, the ESS will want to see the original loan documents as well as documents showing the new balance, or a satisfaction of mortgage, if it was paid in full (ESS Manual 1640.0609.04).

Sometimes it happens that a Community Spouse has assets that belong to her only and the Applicant is denied Medicaid because the Resources of the Community Spouse exceed $92,760. This often happens in a second marriage in which each partner comes to the marriage with his own assets. In such situation, the Community Spouse can refuse to spend-down her Resources saying "I won't spend down. This is my money." This is called the "Just say no" strategy. In legal terms, it is called **Spousal Refusal.** Under federal and state law, the Applicant can still qualify for Medicaid, provided he has no other way to pay for his nursing care, and the Applicant assigns to the State of Florida any right of support he may have from his Community Spouse.

The reader may be thinking that this is all too easy. But it isn't. The Community Spouse will need to cooperate with ESS and prove to them that the Resources belong to her and not to the Applicant. Should the Community spouse refuse spend down, she will not be allowed to keep any part of the Applicant's income. And the Applicant will need to sign CF-ES Form 2504, **ASSIGNMENT OF SUPPORT RIGHTS**. This document gives the state the right to sue the Community Spouse for the support of the Applicant spouse (FAC 65A-1.712, ESS Manual 1640.0314.03, 1640.0119.01, 42 U.S.C. 1396r-5(c)(3)).

It is important to consult with an experienced Elder Law attorney prior to using this option. The attorney will be able to explain what is involved in proving to ESS that the Resources do not belong to the Applicant. He will explain the legal risks involved should the state decide to sue for the support of the institutionalized spouse. Those risks include being responsible to pay for attorney's fees and costs should the Community Spouse lose the law suit.

TOO MUCH RESOURCES — TOO LITTLE INCOME

Suppose the couple with excess Resources has little income. For example, suppose it is determined that the Community Spouse needs at least $2,319 per month, but the couple's combined income is only $1,500. Instead of using the Spousal Refusal strategy, she can ask ESS to allow her to keep as much of their extra Resources as is necessary to give her this minimum income. In effect, she needs to ask ESS "May I keep more than my Resource Allowance so that the income from this property will help to get me to my minimum income?"

It is the legal right of the Community Spouse to receive the minimum income allowance allowed by both state and federal government. It is reasonable to ask ESS to allow her to keep as much of their Resources as necessary to achieve that income, even if it means keeping more than allowed as a Resource Allowance. But it will take an appeal process and the assistance of an experienced Elder Law attorney to convince ESS that allowing her to keep more in Resources is a proper thing to do (FAC 65A-1.712 (4)(e)).

The appeal process can drag on for months. Meanwhile, the status of the Applicant remains in limbo. Because of the legal cost of the appeal and the uncertainty of whether the Court will agree that additional Resources are necessary for the support of the Community Spouse, it may be better to use a spend-down strategy that allows the spouse to receive additional income. One such strategy is the MEDICAID ANNUITY. The Community Spouse uses the excess Resources to buy an annuity that will give her more income each month. This spend-down option is permissible provided it conforms to state and federal law.

A spend-down strategy that is currently allowed by both federal and state law is the of purchase of an *Immediate Pay Annuity*; i.e., an annuity whose payments begin the month after the purchase and continue for a fixed period of time. For purposes of Medicaid eligibility, that fixed period of time must be less than, or equal to, the life expectancy of the Annuitant (in this case, the Community Spouse).

The life expectancy of the Annuitant is determined by referring to the actuarial table as published by the Centers for Medicare and Medicaid Services; State Medicaid Manual, Part 3 (SM3 3259.1) "Life Expectancy Tables — Males and Life Expectancy Tables — Females." You can find excerpts from that table at Public Service Information section of the Eagle Publishing Company Web site.
http://www.eaglepublishing.com

By purchasing an Immediate Pay Annuity, excess Resources can be converted to a monthly income that continues for the term of the policy. The Community Spouse can name someone to receive the Annuity payments in the event she dies before all the payments are made.

In order to qualify as a permissible spend-down strategy, the annuity must meet both state and federal criteria, specifically:

UNASSIGNABLE AND IRREVOCABLE
The annuity contract cannot be transferred, sold or assigned. It must be irrevocable. In other words, nothing can be changed; not the monthly payment, nor the number of payments, nor the identity of the Annuitant.

NO CASH VALUE

The annuity contract must have no value other than the monthly payments to the Annuitant.

ACTUARIALLY SOUND

The annuity contract must be *actuarially sound*, meaning that the money invested in the annuity (plus interest thereon) must be returned to the annuitant during his life expectancy as printed in the State Medicaid Manual (SM3 3259.1) (ESS Manual 1640.0609.02).

There is no rounding "up." For example, according to the State Medicaid Manual a 65 year old man has a life expectancy of 14.96 years. An annuity that makes regular payments to the Annuitant for 14 years is actuarially sound, but an annuity that makes payments for 15 years is not.

We will refer to an annuity that meets all of these criteria (no cash value, unassignable, irrevocable, actuarially sound) as a *Medicaid Annuity*.

 VERIFY THAT THE ANNUITY MEETS STATE CRITERIA PRIOR TO PURCHASE

Once the Annuity is purchased it is irrevocable, so before you buy it, have your Elder Law attorney, or the insurance agent who is selling the Annuity, check with ESS to be sure the Annuity meets state and federal requirements. If you purchase the Annuity and for some reason ESS determines that it does not meet current state and federal criteria, the entire value of the Annuity might count as an impermissible transfer of assets and a Penalty Period of ineligibility will be imposed. The Penalty Period is discussed later in this Chapter.

This spend-down strategy of purchasing a Medicaid Annuity can be used by the Community Spouse even when her income is not a problem. But it may not make economic sense if the sum of her monthly income, including the income from the Annuity, exceeds $2,319. For example, suppose her only income is $1,000 from Social Security, and ESS determines that she needs $2,000 as a Minimum Monthly Maintenance Income Allowance. The ESS will allow her to keep $1,000 of her husband's monthly income. If the Medicaid Annuity pays $1,000 per month (or more), she may keep none of her husband's income. All of his income will be used for his nursing care. In other words, purchasing the Medicaid Annuity may enable the Applicant to qualify for Medicaid, but it may not result in extra income for Community Spouse. And there are other things to consider:

⇨ LOSS OF LIQUIDITY Should the Applicant die shortly after she buys the Annuity, his Spouse cannot cash it in. She must keep the investment for the full term.

⇨ FIXED RETURN ON INVESTMENT Annuities offer a fixed rate of return on the money invested and there is no way to adjust that rate for periods of inflation. The rate of return on the Annuity is set at the time of purchase. We are currently in a period of low interest rates. Should there be a period of high interest rates, the Annuity will still yield the same rate of return as when purchased.

⇨ RISK OF LOSS By purchasing an Annuity, the Community Spouse is giving her money to a company in exchange for the company's promise to pay interest and return part of the principal each month. The company promises to make these payments every month for a certain number of years. Should the company become bankrupt during that period of time, the monies invested might be lost.

Although purchasing a Medicaid Annuity may work for the Community Spouse with a low fixed income, it may not be the best strategy for the single Applicant because any income he receives from the Annuity will be used for his nursing care. One possible exception is the single Applicant who intends to return home after a few months. For example, suppose an unmarried Applicant with $100,000 needs extensive nursing care because of a car accident. If doctors expect that he will be able to return home after several months of therapy and nursing care, he might consider purchasing a Medicaid Annuity for $98,000.

He needs to be concerned that his monthly income does not exceed the current Income Cap, else he will not qualify for Medicaid. Instead of purchasing a Medicaid Annuity that makes equal monthly payments for the term of the Annuity, he might consider purchasing a *Lump-Sum Balloon Style Annuity* that makes relatively small payments each month and a single, large, final payment. Under current Florida law, this type of Medicaid Annuity is permitted, provided the Lump-Sum payment is scheduled to be made during his life expectancy. He can name someone to be the beneficiary of the Annuity should he die before the final Balloon payment is made.

By purchasing the Medicaid Annuity, the Applicant is betting that he will not need nursing care for the rest of his life expectancy. If he loses his bet, then none of his assets are protected. All of his money will be used to pay for his nursing care. In such case, he might better use other options designed for the single Applicant.

Spend-down may not be the best strategy for the single Applicant with significant assets. Sure he can make his funeral arrangements; but that will only use up a small portion of his assets. He could buy an expensive car, but what good would that be if he needs to enter a nursing home? The Medicaid Annuity is a possibility, but if he has a progressive, long-term disease such as Alzheimer's or Parkinson, and needs to go into a facility, he could very well live longer than his life expectancy and all the money invested in the Annuity would be used for his care.

If the Applicant has a medical condition that does not require immediate nursing care, he may decide to simply transfer all of his money to his child. The ESS will consider this to be an *uncompensated transfer,* i.e. the Applicant gets nothing in return for the transfer (love and affection don't count). Should the Applicant go this route, the ESS will impose a *Penalty Period,* i.e., a period of time that the Applicant is disqualified from receiving Medicaid benefits.

Rules relating to the Penalty Period for uncompensated transfers are fairly complex, but in general, the penalty period is computed by dividing the amount transferred by the average monthly cost of nursing home care in the state of Florida. The value for the average monthly cost of nursing care currently being used by the ESS is $3,300. For example, if the Applicant with $100,000 decided to gift the money to his child he would be disqualified for 30 months: $100,000/$3,300 = 30.30 months

The ESS will round this down to 30 months beginning with the month in which the transfer was made (FAC 65A-1.712).

Thirty months is a long time. It could happen that the father needs nursing before the Penalty Period is up. In that case the child will need to return the money so that the father can pay for his nursing care. For example, suppose our Applicant transferred the $100,0000 and six months later he needs nursing care. The Penalty Period for $19,800 of the transferred funds has expired: $3,300 x 6 = $19,800

If the difference ($80,200) is returned to the father, there will be no further Penalty Period. However this is not a complete solution because the father still has too much to qualify for Medicaid. He will need to spend-down his assets (probably on nursing home care) before he can qualify for Medicaid. In such case, the Applicant cannot preserve all of his assets, but he should be able to preserve much of what he owns by making successive gifts to his child.

The strategy is simple. The Applicant enters the nursing home as a private paying patient. Each month he pays for the cost of his care. Each month he makes a gift to his child. The gift must not incur a Penalty Period greater than a single month. Currently, a gift of $6,600 will trigger a two month Penalty Period, so the gift in any given month must be less than that value. For example, if the father gives away $6,500, then there is only a one month penalty:
$$6,500/$3,300 = 1.97 \text{ or } 1 \text{ month}$$

Each month his Resources are reduced by the gift made to his son and the cost of his nursing care. Each month he is disqualified from applying for that month. If he uses $2,500 of his savings each month to pay for the cost of his nursing care and he makes a gift of $6,500 each month to his child, he will reduce his Resources each month by $9,000.

The father should be able to spend down his $80,200 in nine months ($9,000 X 9 = $81,000) with $58,500 going to his son ($6,500 X 9 = $58,500).

 DO IT RIGHT OR SUFFER THE FULL PENALTY

The time of the transfer is critical. The sum total of the gifts made in any given month must not exceed the one month Penalty Period. If the gift periods overlap, or two gifts are made in the same month that add up to more than a one month penalty, the gifts will count as a single transferer with full penalty for that transfer (FAC 65A-1.712).

For example, suppose the gifting of $6,500 starts in May, but the check for May is not cashed until June, ESS will consider that a transfer of $13,000 was made in June. Instead of counting a one month penalty for May and a one month penalty for June, they will impose a 3 month Penalty Period beginning in June and continuing until August: $13,000/$3,300 = 3.94 or 3 months

Best to have an Elder Law attorney supervise the gifting schedule. He will compute the maximum value that you can gift under current values being used for private pay nursing care.

JUST GIVE IT ALL AWAY

The strategy we have been discussing can be used if the Applicant needs nursing care in the near future. But it may happen that a person is diagnosed in the early stages of a progressive disease that is expected to ultimately result in a lengthy stay in a nursing facility. A person in such a situation may decide to give his property away, with the hope that he will not need long term nursing care for at least three years.

The three years is the **Look-back Period** that ESS uses to investigate the finances of a person who applies for Medicaid. The Look-back Period starts on the date the Applicant enters the nursing home and applies for Medicaid and goes back three years from that date. The Look-back Period increases to five years from the date of application if there was a transfer into a Trust (42 U.S.C. 1396p(c); FAC 65A-1.712, ESS Manual 1640.0606, 1640.0607).

If the ESS determines that the Applicant, or his spouse, made transfers during the Look-back Period, the ESS will impose a Penalty Period.

 THERE IS NO LIMIT ON THE PENALTY PERIOD

Although the ESS will only look back three years for transfers, there is no limit on the Penalty Period imposed for that transfer. For example, suppose the Applicant gives his child $300,000. If he applies for Medicaid within three years from the date of transfer, he can be denied Medicaid benefits for seven and a half years.

$$\$300,000 / \$3,300 = 90 \text{ or } 7\,1/2 \text{ years}$$

Of course the way to avoid the problem is to transfer the funds and not apply any sooner than three full years from the date of the transfer. But if the transfer was made into an irrevocable Trust, the Applicant is stuck with the full seven and a half years; because, as discussed, if funds were transferred into a Trust the state has the right to look back 5 years and impose the full penalty for the transfer.

And this is not a game of "Catch me if you can." Under both state and federal law, the Applicant and his spouse (or whoever applies for him) are required to make a full disclosure of transfers made during these periods. Anyone who knowingly and wilfully makes a false statement in an application for Medicaid can be convicted for Medicaid fraud. If the value of the pubic assistance improperly received in any 12 month period exceeds $200, the person who committed the fraud can be convicted of a 3rd degree felony. In addition, the Applicant can be disqualified from receiving further benefits and be required to return all benefits that were paid incorrectly (FS 414.39, 414.41).

The reader may be thinking "Yes, but if I don't make a transfer into a Trust, all the law requires is that I report transfers made within the previous three years. If I come down with an illness that I know will cause me to deteriorate over a period of time, all I need do is give all my money to my child; be sure to wait three years and I will qualify for Medicaid. My child will keep my money safe. Should I need that money, my child will return as much as I need to me. Money that I don't use will be protected for my child."

The Medicaid Qualifying Plan of giving away all assets and then waiting three years is certainly allowed under the law, but this is a "brute force" approach to the problem. There's no finesse. It is a drastic step to take and fraught with peril. Once the money is transferred, a completed gift is made. The child becomes the legal owner of the money and with all of the obvious "what ifs."

What if the child goes bankrupt or dies?

What if the child is sued? Will a Court order the child to use the money you gave to pay the judgment?

What if the child is divorced? Will the Court decide that your child's spouse is entitled to half of that money?

But the real problem is the loss of independence. Being impoverished at a time in your life when you are unable to supplement your income, and when your physical health is declining, can lead to much sadness. Imagine going to your child and asking for money. Imagine the child thinking, or worse yet, asking
          "What's the money for?"

And what if you give the money away and never need nursing care? Medical technology is advancing with amazing speed. Although few cures have been found for mankind's ills, there have been many breakthroughs in their treatment. With modern drugs, many patients are now able to function without the need for long-term care. Even those who have been diagnosed with a progressive disease may not need nursing care for several years — maybe never.

Meanwhile, the money is gone, and your independence along with it.

Giving all one's money away and then waiting three years works, but at the cost of your independence. Putting money into an irrevocable Trust and waiting five years has its risks. A lot can happen during that time. You could require full nursing care the day after you transfer your assets into the Trust. Maybe the five year Look-back is changed to a six year Look-back period.

For those in good health, an alternative is to do nothing until you actually need nursing home care and then implement a Medicaid qualifying strategy at that time. Of course there is the chance that you take suddenly ill, say with a stroke, and are unable to implement a Medicaid Qualifying plan. A properly drafted Durable Power Of Attorney should solve the problem. You can appoint your spouse or child to be your Agent to do so for you.

It is important that the Durable Power of Attorney be properly drafted by an Elder Law attorney. In December 2002, A New Jersey Court refused to allow a son to transfer property on behalf of his incapacitated mother for the purpose of qualifying for Medicaid. Although his mother gave him a Power of Attorney authorizing him to apply for Medicaid on her behalf, the Court refused to allow the transfer because the Power of Attorney ". . . did not provide for him to make gifts on her behalf to himself or anyone else, either to qualify her for Medicaid or for any other reason" (*In the Matter of Mildred Keri*, Superior Court of New Jersey, Appellate Division, A-5949-01T5).

This is also the case in Florida. The Power of Attorney must grant specific authority to transfer property otherwise the transfer is not valid (*James v. James*, 843 So.2d 304 (Fla. App. 5 Dist. 2003).

CAUTION THE ONLY THING CERTAIN IS CHANGE

The discussion relating to Medicaid Qualifying Plans for the state of Florida is not intended to lull the reader into a false sense of security. The only thing certain about state and federal laws is that they will change. Whatever strategy you choose may not be around when you need it. For example, there are those who oppose the use of the Medicaid Annuity. Legislation has been proposed in

Florida that will make the purchase of a Lump-Sum Balloon Style Annuity an impermissible transfer. If the law is passed, a purchase of this type of Annuity will subject the Applicant to a Penalty Period.

More importantly, there is a proposal in the current administration to give states new powers to reduce, eliminate or increase Medicaid benefits within the state. Under this proposal, benefits for welfare recipients, poor children and other groups who are automatically eligible for Medicaid would remain regulated by federal law. The state would be given autonomy to administer the Medicaid program for other groups; and in particular for the elderly in need of nursing care. Proponents of state autonomy explain that with autonomy, the state could increase benefits, but in these days of budget deficits, more likely the states will opt to decrease Medicaid benefits to the elderly. If the states are given autonomy in administering the long-term nursing care program, there would no longer be uniformity imposed by current federal statutes. Medicaid benefits for the elderly could vary significantly state to state.

Not only would there be variation state to state, but there could be variation within the state. State programs could be administered with different eligibility criteria county to county. There could even be a difference in benefits county to county.

The point is that there is no certainty when it comes to future Medicaid qualifying options.

But we did not write this chapter to give the reader a definitive Medicaid Qualifying strategy. Rather it was to give the reader an understanding of the law as it relates to qualifying for Medicaid; and to let the reader know that under current law, options are available should the need for long-term nursing care arise in the future.

We also wrote this chapter to let the general public understand how this federal program is currently administered here in the state of Florida. And, incidentally, we touched only on the basics. There are other, more sophisticated, Medicaid Qualifying options available that an experienced Elder Law attorney can explain to you. The prudent thing to do is to visit an Elder Law attorney if and when you become concerned about a long term care problem. He can explain current law to you as it relates to qualifying for Medicaid. He can suggest the best path for you to follow, given your set of circumstances.

It is also important to keep up with changes in policy both in the state and federal government; and to let your legislators know how you feel about such changes.

Protecting the Homestead 11

We discussed the problem of having cash assets in excess of that allowed under current federal and state law; but what about the person whose only asset of value is his home? As explained in Chapter 10, whether the home counts as an asset for purposes of qualifying for Medicaid depends on whether his spouse or dependent family member is occupying the home. Even if no family member occupies the home, the Applicant cannot be denied Medicaid benefits because he owns a home, provided he says he intends to return to his home. However, once he receives Medicaid benefits, the state has the right to have a physician determine whether the Recipient can reasonably be expected to return home within a year. If not, the state has a right to place a lien on the property for monies spent on his behalf.

Even if the state does not place a lien on his home during his lifetime, if the Medicaid Recipient received Medical Assistance after the age of 55, the state can seek recovery from the sale of his home once the home is sold or he dies (42 U.S.C.A. 1396p(b)(1)(B)). The state will not seek recovery from a home owned by the Recipient while his spouse, or minor or disabled child there. However, once the child reaches 21, or the spouse and disabled child are deceased, whoever inherits the home will need to pay off that lien or the state can force the sale of the property and take the money from the proceeds of the sale of the house (42 CFR 433.36, FS 409.9101).

In this chapter we discuss ways to protect the home from such a *Medicaid Lien*.

Protecting the homestead is easy to do if the Medicaid Recipient is married. Under state and federal law, the Applicant can transfer his home to the Community Spouse without penalty. He can make the transfer either before or after he applies for Medicaid (42 U.S.C. 1396p (c) 2A, ESS Manual 1640.0609.03, 1640.0610).

If the home is in the name of the Medicaid Recipient only, he can sign a deed transferring the property to his spouse. If he and the Community Spouse own the property jointly, or as Tenants By The Entirety, they can sign a deed transferring the property to the Community Spouse. It is important to make the transfer because the property would be in the Applicant's name only in the event the Community Spouse died first. In such case, the property would be available to reimburse the state for monies spent.

Protecting the homestead is more of a problem for the aged, single parent; and it is a problem for aging parents both of whom are not in the best of health. Who knows which of them will require long term nursing care? Maybe both will need such care. Maybe neither of them will require nursing care. Most parents want to have their children inherit the one thing the parent has of value, namely their home. Parents fear that if they ever need Medicaid benefits, their home will be sold to reimburse the state. This idea is so distressing to some parents that even though they are in relatively good health, they may decide to transfer their home to their child with the understanding that the parents will continue to live there for the rest of their lives. Those planning such a move need to understand that they are trading one risk (need to apply for Medicaid) for several other risks.

⊠ RISK OF LOSS

Once you transfer the property to your child it becomes his property and that property can be lost or used to pay for his debts just like anything else he owns. Your child could run into serious financial difficulties. Your child could be sued. This is especially a risk if your child is a professional (doctor, nurse, accountant, financial planner, attorney, etc.). If your child is found to be personally liable for damages, your home could become part of the settlement of that law suit.

If your child is (or gets) married, then this complicates matters even more. If the child divorces, the value of your home might be included as part of the property settlement agreement. This may be to your child's detriment because the child may need to share the value of the property with his/her former spouse. If you do not transfer the property, it cannot become part of his marital equation.

Even if your child is single there is a risk of loss. Your child may want to take out a business loan. It the loan is significant, the lender will want to include everything your child owns as collateral (security for the debt). If the lender learns that you are occupying the house, he will especially want to include your house as collateral because that will motivate your son to repay the loan.

The point is, transferring the house to your child could be bad for both of you. And that is not the only downside.

⊠ LOSS OF HOMESTEAD CREDITOR PROTECTION

Your homestead is a protected asset. With the exception of property taxes and the loan on your homestead, none of your creditors can force the sale of your property (Florida Constitution, Article X, Section 4).

If you simply transfer your homestead to a child, you lose your homestead protection against creditors. If you are married, it is a double loss of creditor protection. Not only do you lose creditor protection for yourself, you lose it for your spouse and children as well (see Chapter 5).

If your child does not occupy that property as his homestead, then there is no homestead creditor protection whatsoever. The child's creditors can force the sale of the property (that's your home) for relatively small amounts of unpaid debts.

⊠ LOSS OF HOMESTEAD TAX CREDIT

Every homeowner whose permanent residence is in the state of Florida is entitled to a homestead tax exemption. Additional exemptions are allowed for any number of reasons such as the owner being a widow, or widower, or blind or permanently disabled. If you transfer your homestead, you will lose your right to receive these significant tax breaks (FS 196.031, 196.101, 196.202).

⊠ POSSIBLE GIFT TAX

A Gift Tax needs to be paid if the value of the equity in your home — plus the value of all the gifts you gave over your lifetime in excess of the Annual Gift Tax Exclusion, exceeds the lifetime Gift Tax Exclusion. The current lifetime Gift Tax Exclusion is $1,000,000, so for most of us, this is not a problem. Yet there still is the hassle of filing a Gift Tax return.

⊠ POSSIBLE CAPITAL GAINS TAX

Although Congress has expressed its intent to phase out the Estate Tax, there is no discussion to do away with the Capital Gains Tax. If you gift the property to the child during your lifetime, when he sells the property he will pay a Capital Gains Tax on the increase in value from the price you paid for your home to the selling price at the time your child sells the property.

If you do not make the gift during your lifetime, the child will inherit the property with a step-up in basis, i.e., he will inherit the property at its market value as of the date of your death. Under today's tax structure and continuing until 2009, that step-up in basis is unlimited. If your child sells the property when he inherits it, he will pay no Capital Gains Tax, regardless of how large the step-up in basis.

In 2010, there will be a limit on the amount that can be inherited free of the Capital Gains Tax but that limit is quite high so for most of us this is not a concern.

⊠   POSSIBLE LOSS OF GOVERNMENT BENEFITS

If you are married and you transfer property to someone other than your spouse, then depending upon the value of the transfer, both you and your spouse could be disqualified from receiving Medicaid or Supplemental Security Income ("SSI") if you apply within three years from the date of transfer of the property. That increases to five years if you transfer the property into a Trust. It could happen that during that period of time, one of you takes suddenly ill and requires long-term nursing care.

Why jeopardize your right to receive Medicaid for both of you? Owning a homestead will not disqualify you from receiving Medicaid, but transferring it may make you and your spouse ineligible for a long time.

The elderly parent, who is single, may not be convinced that gifting the house is a bad idea. He may be thinking "By giving my home to my child, I risk not being able to qualify for Medicaid for three years. If I don't make the gift and need Medicaid at any time during the rest of my lifetime, the state will get the house for sure."

But there are better Estate Plans than the outright gift. The Life Estate strategy may be one of them.

You can give the property to your child, and keep a Life Estate for yourself. Your child will have no right to your homestead while you are alive so you have no fear that the property can be lost or taken from you during your lifetime. Upon your death, your child will own the property 100%, and without the need for Probate.

Depending on the value of your home, this Life Estate approach might allow you to shorten the Medicaid transfer Penalty Period, because you are not giving your child the full value of your home, you are just giving away the value of the **Remainder Interest** i.e., what is left of the property after your death.

The value of the Remainder Interest depends on your life expectancy. A gift of a Remainder Interest when you are 90 is worth more to your child than when you are 50.

DETERMINING THE VALUE OF THE REMAINDER INTEREST
The Centers for Medicare and Medicaid Services publishes a table of values for the Life Estate Interest and the Remainder Interest based on the age of the Grantor at the time of the transfer (State Medicaid Manual, Part 3 (SM3 3258.9) LIFE ESTATE AND REMAINDER INTEREST TABLE). You can find excerpts from this table, at the Public Information section of the Eagle Publishing Company Web site.   http://www.eaglepublishing.com

Fortunately, this table goes up to age 109, so the value they assign to the remainder interest is relatively low. For example, according to this table, if a 70 year old makes a transfer to his son and keeps a Life Estate for himself, his Life Estate is equal to 61% of the value of the property. The remainder interest is worth only 39%.

The actual percentage given in the table for the Remainder Interest is .39478. If the father's equity in the home** is $100,000 it means the value of the gift of the Remainder Interest is $39,478 (ESS Manual 1640.0551). This greatly reduces the Penalty Period. If he transferred the house and did not keep a Life Estate, his penalty period would be 30 months: $100,000/$3,300 = 30.30 or 30 months

** fair market value less monies owed on the property

By keeping a Life Estate that Penalty Period reduces to 11 months: $39,478/$3,300 = 11.96 or 11 months. Should he apply for Medicaid after the 11 month Penalty Period, the ESS will not count his Life Estate interest as a Resource. However, should he need institutional nursing care and rent out the property in his absence, the rental income will count as income to the Medicaid Recipient (FAC 65A-1.712).

 THE LIFE ESTATE IS NOT
A COMPLETE SOLUTION

A Life Estate is a better Medicaid Qualifying Plan than an outright gift but only for purposes of shortening the period of ineligibility. Issues of control and taxes and recovery still remain.

CONTROL
You will not be able to sell your home without permission from your child.

TAX ISSUES
And, as explained at the end of Chapter 2, if you sell the home, you might need to pay a Capital Gains Tax.

RECOVERY BY THE STATE

Under Federal law, the state has the right to recover monies spent on your behalf if you received nursing care under Medicaid after the age of 55. Monies can be recovered from property you owned at the time of your death. This includes property you own jointly with another, and property in which you own a Life Estate interest (42 U.S.C. 1396p(b)(4)(B)).

As of this writing, the state of Florida has not sought recovery from property in which the Medicaid Recipient owned a Life Estate interest. But the law is on the books and state policy could change in the future.

Before you decide to transfer your home to your child and keep a Life Estate for yourself, it is important to check with an Elder Law attorney to investigate the full consequences of the transfer.

TRANSFERS THAT PROTECT

The most important reason not to transfer the homestead is that it is an Exempt Property for purposes of becoming eligible for Medicaid. However, there is still the concern that after you become eligible for Medicaid, the state will place a Medicaid Lien on your homestead for monies spent on your behalf. Under current law, there are several ways to protect your home from such lien. For a married person, the home can be protected by transferring it to the Community Spouse.

TRANSFERRING THE HOME TO THE SPOUSE

As explained, the Applicant is free to transfer his home to his spouse either before or after he qualifies for Medicaid. However, because of our unique Florida laws, even though the Community Spouse has title to the home, the Medicaid Recipient still has a Life Estate interest in the property. (see page 34) — with all of the inherent problems discussed on the previous page. The solution is to have the couple sign a post-nuptial agreement with the Applicant giving up his Life Estate interests. An Elder Law attorney should be able to draft the post-nuptial agreement and the deed transferring the property to the spouse.

Things become complicated if the Applicant is too ill to sign these documents, and he did not sign a Power of Attorney giving someone authority to transfer property that he owns. In that case, it may be necessary to have a Guardian appointed who can ask the Court for permission to make the transfer. The downside is that guardianships are expensive to establish and maintain, and there is no guarantee that the judge will allow the transfer of the homestead to the Community Spouse.

TRANSFERRING THE HOME TO A SIBLING

Under state and federal law, if an Applicant owns his home together with a sibling and the sibling lived with the Applicant for at least one year before entering the nursing facility, then the Applicant can transfer the home to the sibling without a Medicaid transfer penalty (42 U.S.C. 1396p, ESS Manual 1640.0609.03).

This law presents an opportunity for an unmarried Applicant who has a brother or sister to protect the homestead. The only question is how the sibling becomes co-owner. If the Applicant and his sibling purchased the property together, and the sibling lived in the home for a year prior to the Applicant entering the nursing home, then the sibling's interest in the property is protected. The Applicant can transfer his share of the homestead to his sibling without penalty, and that will protect all of the homestead.

If the house is in the Applicant's name only, then it is important to consult with an Elder Law attorney to determine the best way for the sibling to become part owner of the home. Federal law only requires that the sibling have an *equity interest* in the property. An equity interest could be joint ownership or a Tenancy In Common or a Remainder Interest in the homestead. An Elder Law attorney will be able to suggest a method of transferring an equity interest to the sibling that will result in a Penalty Period of a year or less. The attorney will also assist with preparing documentation to present to ESS to verify that:

⇨　the sibling owns an equity interest in the home

⇨　the Penalty Period for the transfer has passed

⇨　the sibling occupied the home for a year prior to the Applicant entering the nursing home.

A similar law applies to the Medicaid recipient who owns his home and wants to transfer it to his child. The federal law allows a transfer of the homestead to the child without penalty, provided the child lived with and took care of his parent for at least two years before the parent entered the nursing home.

There is no requirement that the child own an equity interest in the property; but the federal statute does require that the state verify that the child lived in the home and provided care to the parent for the two years; and that this care enabled the parent to remain at home rather than be placed in a nursing home (42 U.S.C. 1396p(c)(2)(A)(iv), ESS Manual 1640.0609.03).

If the value of the house is not greater than the two year Penalty Period it may be just as easy to transfer the home to the child and wait out the two years. Specifically, a transfer of $79,200 will result in a two year penalty period.
$$\$3,300 \times 24 = \$79,200$$

If the parent's equity in the home is worth no more than $79,200, the home can be transferred to the child without the need for the child to prove to ESS that care was given to the parent over that two year period.

If the home is worth significantly more, then it is important to consult with an Elder Law attorney, preferably prior to the two year period. The attorney will explain how to document that care over the two year period so that the information can be presented to the ESS when the parent applies for Medicaid.

Some of the things ESS will want to know are:

⇒ the Applicant's medical condition during the two year period

⇒ whether the child lived in the home for the required time period

⇒ what care was provided by the child that enabled the parent to remain at home rather than being placed in an institution

⇒ how many hours per day were spent by the child in caring for his parent

⇒ whether the child worked outside of the home during the two year period; and if so, who cared for the parent while the child was at work.

The ESS may want a friend or family member to verify that the child did provide the necessary care during the two years.

Once it is established by ESS that federal requirements are satisfied, the property can be transferred to the child without affecting the right of the Applicant to receive Medicaid benefits.

The Applicant or his spouse may transfer their homestead to their minor child (under the age of 21) without penalty. They are also allowed to transfer the homestead to a child (minor or adult) who is blind, or disabled. In the event that the child does not have a determination of blindness or disability from the Social Security Administration, the ESS will review the child's medical records to determine whether the child is blind or disabled

If the child is receiving Social Security disability benefits, the parent can transfer money to a Special Needs Trust for the child (see Chapter 7). This transfer will not disqualify the child (or the parent) from receiving government benefits, provided the Trust is drafted according to state and federal law (42 U.S.C. 1396p(c)(2A), ESS Manual 1640.0609.03, 1640.0609.04).

CAUTION DON'T TRY THIS ON YOUR OWN

A Medicaid Qualifying Plan is not something to attempt on your own. The Medicaid program is complex and volatile. There are many levels of law that govern Medicaid. There are the federal statutes (Social Security Act Title XIX/P.L. 89-97); the U.S. Code of Federal Regulations (42 CFR 430-435) and the Centers for Medicare and Medicaid Services State Medicaid Manual, Part 3 that say how the federal statutes are to be administered in the United States.

There are the Florida Medicaid statutes (Chapter 409 Social and Economic Assistance); and the Florida Administrative Code (Chapters 65A-1, 65A-2, 65A-4) explaining how the plan is to be administered in the state of Florida. That's four levels of rules and regulations that are constantly changing — often with little or no notice to the general public.

And the laws are not well written.
In *Rehabilitation Association of Virginia v. Kozlowski*, 42 F.3d 1444, 1450 (4th Cir 1994), the Court had nothing but sympathy for officials who must interpret or administer these laws. "There can be no doubting that the statutes and provisions in question, involving the financing of Medicare and Medicaid, are among the most completely impenetrable texts within human experience. Indeed, one approaches them . . . with dread, for not only are they dense reading of the most tortuous kind, but Congress also revisits the area frequently, generously cutting and pruning in the process and making any solid grasp of the matters addressed merely a passing phase."

Judges in the federal District Court were equally critical: "The Social Security Act is among the most intricate ever drafted by Congress. Its Byzantine construction ... makes the Act 'almost unintelligible to the uninitiated.' ... The District Court ... described the Medicaid statute as 'an aggravated assault on the English language, resistant to attempts to understand it'." (*Schweiker v. Gray Panthers*, 453 U.S. 34(1981)).

Most states have a manual that they provide to workers who are in charge of implementing the Medicaid Program. In Florida, that manual is the Economic Self-Sufficiency Program Policy Manual. But even Manual instructions are complex and subject to different interpretations. For example, ESS Manual 1640.0563 states "For institutional care . . . applicants with community spouses, all personal property is excluded . . ." Yet 1640.0565.02 goes on to say "Household goods and personal effect items valued at more than $500 are included as an asset." The Manual does not say whether the $500 limit applies only to the single Applicant, so the ESS in one county may count personal items worth more than $500, regardless of whether the Applicant is married. In another county, ESS may reason that since 1640.0565.02 comes after 1640.0563, so it is implied that the $500 limit is for single Applicants only.

It is not surprising that what may be an acceptable Medicaid qualifying option in one county, may be challenged by the ESS in another county. If the ESS decides to challenge a particular strategy, even though that strategy is based on federal or state law, you will have no choice but to appeal the ruling.

THE MEDICAID APPEAL

An Applicant who is denied Medicaid benefits will receive notice from ESS that he has the right to appeal. The first step in the appeal process is for the Applicant, or someone acting on his behalf, to request a "Fair Hearing." Once requested, a Hearing Officer will be appointed to conduct the hearing and decide the matter. The Hearing Officer is an employee of the Department of Children and Family Services who was not involved in the initial determination. And the Hearing Officer cannot be the immediate supervisor of the Economic Self-Sufficiency Specialist who made the decision.

Although the hearing is conducted in an informal manner, it is, none-the-less, a complex legal proceeding. The Department of Children and Family Services will be represented by a District Representative. The District Representative will present evidence and quote laws that support the ruling of the ESS. To win the appeal, the Applicant, or his representative, needs a complete understanding of all applicable law. He must be ready to present evidence, and perhaps call witnesses to support his position. The Applicant also needs to know the correct legal procedure to discover (find out) what information the District Representative intends to present at the hearing (FAC 65-2.045, 65-2.057, 65-2.058, ESS Manual 0640.0121, 0640.0122).

Few Applicants have the necessary knowledge and skills to adequately represent their side of the argument, so it is important to employ an attorney who is familiar with the law and skilled at presenting evidence that will support the position of the Applicant. Those who cannot afford to employ an attorney, should ask Legal Aid for assistance (see page ix).

If the Applicant has been denied Medicaid coverage, more likely than not, the Hearing Officer will rule in favor of ESS, because under Florida law, the burden of proof is on the Applicant. This means that the District Representative is not required to prove that ESS was right, but rather it is the Applicant's job to convince the Hearing Officer that ESS was wrong. Not an easy thing to do.

If the Applicant loses at this administrative level, he can take the case before a Florida District Court of Appeal. The District Court of Appeal will take a broader look at the picture and consider state and federal law, as well as the Constitutional rights of the Applicant (Florida Constitution, Section 4(b)(1)), FAC 65-2.066, 65-2.060, ESS Manual 0640.0125, 0640.0123). If the Applicant is turned down in the District Court of Appeal, he can appeal to a federal court — all the way up to the United States Supreme Court.

The appeal process is expensive, stressful and time consuming. In Chapter 10 we presented may different options that are available to the Applicant at this time. It is better to choose a Medicaid Qualifying strategy that the ESS in your county has allowed in the past, even if it is not the very best Medicaid Qualifying Plan for you. An experienced Elder Law attorney can explain what Medicaid qualifying strategies have been allowed in the past in your county and which strategies are likely to be challenged.

Guiding Those You Love 12

Once you are satisfied with your Estate Plan, then the final thing to consider is whether your heirs will be able to locate your assets after you're gone.

Most people have their business records in one place, their Will in another place, car titles and deeds in still another place. When someone dies, their beneficiaries may feel as if they are playing a game of "hide and seek" with the decedent. The game might be fun were it not for the fact that unlocated items may be forever lost. For example, suppose you die in an accident and no one knows you are insured by your credit card company for accidental death in the amount of $25,000. The only one to profit is the insurance company, which is just that much richer because no one told them that you died as a result of an accident.

And how about a key to a safe deposit box? Will anyone find it? Even if they find the key, how will they locate the box?

It is not difficult to arrange things so that your affairs are always in order. It amounts to being aware of what you own (and owe) and keeping a record of your possessions. A side benefit is that by doing so, you will always know where all your business records are. If you ever spent time trying to collect information to file your taxes or trying to find a lost stock or bond certificate, you will appreciate the value of organizing your records.

POINTING THE WAY

Heirs need all the help they can get. It is difficult enough dealing with the loss, without the frustration of trying to locate important documents. Your heirs will have no problem locating your assets if you keep all of your records in a single place. It can be a desk drawer or a file cabinet or even a shoe box. It is helpful if you keep a separate file or folder for each type of investment. You might consider setting up the following folders:

☐ THE BANK & SECURITIES FOLDER

Store your original certificates for stocks, bonds, mutual funds, certificates of deposit, in a folder labeled BANK & SECURITIES FOLDER. In addition to the original certificate include a copy of the contract you signed with each financial institution. The contract will show where you have funds and who you named as beneficiary or joint owner of the account. If someone owes you money and has signed a promissory note or mortgage that identifies you as the lender, then you can store these documents in this folder as well.

If you wish to store your original documents in a safe deposit box, then keep a record of the location of the safe deposit box, and the number of the box, in this folder. Make a copy of all of the items stored in the box and place the copies in this folder. If you have an extra key to the box, then put the key in the folder. If you are the only person with access to the box, it may take a Probate procedure to remove items from the box once you die. Consider giving someone you trust the right to gain entry to the box in the event of your incapacity or death.

📁 THE INSURANCE FOLDER

The INSURANCE FOLDER is for each insurance policy that you own, be it life insurance, car insurance, homeowner's insurance or a health care insurance. If you purchased real property, you may have received a title commitment at closing and the original title insurance policy some weeks later when you received your original deed from recording. If you cannot locate the title insurance policy, then contact the closing agent and have them send you a copy of your title insurance policy.

📁 THE PENSION AND ANNUITY FOLDER

Put all of the documents relating to your pension or annuity in this folder. Include the telephone number and/or address of the person to contact in the event of your death.

FOR FEDERAL RETIREES

If you are a Federal Retiree, you should have received your **PERSONAL IDENTIFICATION NUMBER (PIN)** and the person who will inherit your pension (your *survivor annuitant*) should have received his/her own PIN as well. It is relatively simple to obtain this during your lifetime, but it may be difficult and/or stressful for your survivor annuitant to work through the system once you are gone.

Survivor annuitant benefits are not automatic. Your survivor annuitant must apply for them by submitting a death claim to the Office of Personnel Management. Your survivor needs to know that it is necessary to apply and also how to apply. You can call the Office of Personnel Management at (888) 767-6738 to get printed information that you can keep in this folder to guide your survivor annuitant through the process. You can also download information from their Web site: http://www.opm.gov

🗁 THE DEED FOLDER

Many people save every scrap of paper associated with the closing of real property. If you closed recently on real estate and there was a mortgage involved in the purchase, you probably walked away from closing with enough paper to wallpaper your kitchen. If you wish, you can keep all of those papers in a separate file that identifies the property, for example:

CLOSING PAPERS FOR THE TAMPA PROPERTY

Place the original deed (or a copy if the original is in a safe deposit box) in a separate DEED FOLDER. Include cemetery deeds, condominium deeds, timesharing certificates, deed to out of state property, etc. Also include a copy of related documents such as an Abstract of Title, or a recorded condominium approval. If you have a title insurance policy, put the original in the insurance folder, and a copy in this folder. If you have a mortgage on your property, put a copy of the recorded mortgage and promissory note in a separate LIABILITY FOLDER. Once the mortgage is paid off, the lender should give you Satisfaction of Mortgage. The Satisfaction needs to be recorded. You can keep the recorded Satisfaction together with the deed to the property.

LOCATING REAL PROPERTY

If you own a vacant lot, your beneficiaries will find the deed (or a copy) in this folder but that deed will not contain the address of that property because it doesn't have one. The post office does not assign a street address until there is a building on the site. Your beneficiary could get the location of the property from city or county records. But why make things hard for them? Include a simple handwritten note in this folder that tells them exactly how to locate the property.

☞ THE TAX RECORD FOLDER

Your Personal Representative (or next of kin) will need to file your final income tax returns. Keep a copy of your tax returns (both federal and state) for the past three years in your Tax Record Folder. As explained in Chapter 3, beginning in 2010, there will be a cap on the step-up basis to 4.3 million dollars for property inherited by your spouse and 1.3 million for property inherited by anyone else. It is important to keep a record of the basis of your property, not only for your heirs, but for yourself should you decide to sell the property during your lifetime. If you purchase real property, you need to keep a record of the purchase price as well as monies you paid to improve the property. You need these records to determine whether a Capital Gains Tax is due on the transfer. Your accountant can help you set up a bookkeeping system to keep a running record of your basis in everything you own of value.

☞ THE LIABILITY FOLDER

The LIABILITY FOLDER should contain all loan documents of debts that you owe. For example, if you purchased real property and have a mortgage on that property, put a copy of the mortgage and promissory note in this folder. If you owe money on a car, put the loan documents here. A lease is a liability, because you have contracted to pay a certain amount for the period of the lease, so include a copy of any lease agreement in this Liability Folder. If you have a credit card, put a copy of the contract you signed with the credit card company in this folder.

Many people never take the time to calculate their net worth (what a person owns less what that person owes). By having a record of your assets and outstanding debts, you can calculate your net worth whenever you wish.

🗀 THE PERSONAL PROPERTY FOLDER

MOTOR VEHICLES

Put all motor vehicle titles in a Personal Property Folder. This includes cars, mobile homes, boats, planes, etc. If you owe money on the vehicle, the lender may have possession of the title certificate. If such is the case, then put a copy of the title certificate and registration in this folder and a copy of the loan documents in a separate liability folder. If you own a boat or plane, then identify the location of the motor vehicle. For example, if you are leasing space in an airplane hangar or in a marina, keep a copy of the leasing agreement in this folder.

JEWELRY

If you own expensive jewelry, keep a picture of the item together with the sales receipt or written appraisal in this folder.

COLLECTOR'S ITEMS

If you own a valuable art or coin collection, or any other item of significant value, include a picture of the item in this folder. Also include evidence of ownership of the item, such as a sales receipt or a certificate of authenticity, or a written appraisal of the property.

🗀 THE PERSONAL RECORDS FOLDER

The PERSONAL RECORDS FOLDER should include documents that relate to you personally, such as a birth certificate, naturalization papers, marriage certificate, divorce papers, military records, social security card; etc.

🗁 THE ESTATE PLANNING DOCUMENT FOLDER

WILL/TRUST
Place your Will and/or Trust in a separate folder. If your attorney has your original Will, then make a note of that fact together with a copy of the Will. If the original document is in a safe deposit box, then place a copy of the document in this folder together with instructions about how to find the original.

It is important to keep a copy of your Will or Trust because over the years you may forget what provision you made. Keeping a copy in your home may save you the time and effort to retrieve the document, just to determine whether it needs to be updated.

PRENUPTIAL/POSTNUPTIAL AGREEMENT
Prenuptial or postnuptial agreements usually provide for the disposition of your property upon your death, so a copy of the agreement should be included in this folder.

OTHER ESTATE PLANNING DOCUMENTS
You can include the original or a copy of your Power of Attorney, Designation of Health Care Surrogate or Preneed Funeral Plan, in this folder.

Many do not have the time, nor inclination, to "play" with all these folders. They do not anticipate an immediate demise. Getting hit by a truck, or dying in a fiery plane crash is not something to think about, much less prepare for. But consider that death is not the only problem. You could take suddenly ill (say with a stroke) and become incapacitated. Even the most time-starved optimist should have a murmur of concern that his loved ones will be left with a mess should something unforeseen happen.

If you do not feel like doing a complete job of organizing your records at this time, consider an abridged version. You can set up a single folder and place all of your important papers in that folder. You need to make the folder easily accessible to whoever you wish to manage your affairs in the event of your incapacity or death. You can do this by letting that person know of the existence of the folder and how to get it in an emergency.

You can keep the folder in an easily accessed place in your home with the folder identified as containing important papers. We labeled it "THE QUICK-FIND FOLDER" because the folder gives you and your family easy access to important information and/or documents. But you can create your own heading such as: "MY IMPORTANT PAPERS" or if you want a particular person to access the folder, you might label it: "RECORDS FOR MY SON, ROBERT"

It is helpful if you include a list of all you own and the location of each item in that folder.

WHEN TO UPDATE YOUR ESTATE PLAN

We discussed people's natural disinclination to make an Estate Plan until they are faced with their own mortality. Many believe that they will make just one Will and then die (maybe that's why they put off making a Will). The reality is, most people who make a Will change it at least once before they die. If you have an Estate Plan, it is important to update it when any of the following events take place:

✍ CHANGE IN MARITAL STATUS

If you marry or divorce, there are certain changes that take place by law. For example, once you divorce, all property that you own as a Tenant by the Entirety becomes property owned as Tenants In Common (FS 689.15) If you divorce and then die without getting around to changing your Will, any provision that you made for your former spouse in the document will be read as if your former spouse died before you (FS 732.507).

But it is important to not just rely on the law. Best to change all documents after a divorce or separation. This includes your Designation of Health Care Surrogate, Durable Power of Attorney, bank accounts, deeds, insurance policies, etc.

NOTIFY EMPLOYER OF CHANGE

If you change your marital status (either marry or divorce) you need to tell your employer of the change so that the employer can change your status for purposes of paycheck tax deductions. If you have a health insurance plan or a pension plan, that provides benefits to your spouse, then these need to be changed as well.

✍ A CHANGE IN RELATIONSHIP

Getting married, separated or divorced; having a child; having a beneficiary of your Estate die, are all profound changes in one's life. When the dust settles, it is important to examine your Estate Plan to see if it needs revision. If you have a Trust, you can change it by having your attorney prepare an *amendment* to the Trust. If you have a Will, your attorney can prepare a *codicil* (a supplement) to the Will.

It is important to have changes made by a properly drafted and signed document. If you make changes by crossing things out or writing over your Will, or Trust, the validity of the document can be challenged once you die. If you simply rip up the old Will, that will effectively revoke the Will (FS 732.506). But it could happen that someone (perhaps your attorney) has a copy of the Will. If no one knows that you revoked the Will, they may think the Will is lost and then offer the copy of the Will for Probate. If you draft a new Will, the first paragraph should say, "I revoke all prior Wills ..." This makes it clear that you want the new Will to replace all other Wills.

 ### NEW SPOUSE OR CHILD CAN CHALLENGE OLD WILL

CHALLENGE BY SURVIVING SPOUSE

If you marry and "forget" to change a Will you prepared prior to your marriage, then your spouse can challenge your Will unless:

➪ you provided for your spouse in your Will - or -

➪ your Will shows that it was your intent not to provide for your future spouse - or -

➪ your spouse signs a prenuptial or postnuptial agreement giving up the right to inherit your property (FS 732.301).

If your spouse successfully challenges the Will you prepared before the marriage, he/she is entitled to receive as much as he/she would have received had you died without a Will (FS 732.301).

CHALLENGE BY AFTERBORN CHILD
Similarly, a child born or adopted after you prepared your Will is entitled to as much as he/she would have received had you died without a Will, unless:

⇨ you gave that intestate share to you child prior to your death, and there is evidence that the gift was given in place of an inheritance - or -

⇨ the Will indicates that the omission was intentional; i.e., that you wanted to omit any later born or adopted from inheriting your property - or -

⇨ you had one or more children when you made your Will and the Will gives all your property to your surviving spouse who is the parent of the omitted child (FS 732.302).

If your spouse or child is successful in challenging your Will, the beneficiaries of your Will need to contribute part of their inheritance to make up that share. This could lead to disagreements and hard feelings for those forced to contribute. It is better that you change your Will after you marry or have a child, so that the beneficiaries of your Will receive no more and no less than you intended.

BENEFICIARY MOVES OR DIES

Most people remember to name an alternate beneficiary should one of their beneficiaries die. But how many of us remember to notify the pension plan or insurance company when a beneficiary moves?

It is important that your beneficiary's address be available to those in charge of distributing funds upon your death. Many life insurance proceeds are never paid because the company cannot locate the beneficiary. The Actuarial Office of the Federal Employees' Group Life Insurance Program reported that as of October, 2001, they had over 40 million dollars in unpaid benefits, mostly because they could not locate the beneficiary at the last given address.

RELOCATION TO A NEW STATE OR COUNTRY

There is no need to change your Estate Plan for a move within the state of Florida. There is much to check out if you are moving to another state. If your attorney has your original Will (or any other original document), then unless you plan to continue with him as your attorney, you need to retrieve those items and take them with you to the new state.

You need to determine whether your Will conforms to the laws of the state of your new residence. Most states will honor a Will drafted according to Florida law, however, the rights of a spouse vary considerably state to state. If you are married and have not provided the minimum amount as required by the laws of the new state, then should you die before your spouse, your Will may be challenged on that basis. The same applies to a Trust. Many states, like Florida, require funds from a Revocable Living Trust be used to pay the minimum amount allowed by law to the surviving spouse.

LAWS OF INTESTATE SUCCESSION

If you do not have a Will, then it is important to check out the Laws of Intestate Succession for that state. In some states they are referred to as the *Laws of Descent and Distribution.* Each state has its own laws relating to the inheritance of property and those laws are very different from each other. Who has the right to inherit your property in the state of Florida may be different from who can inherit your property in another state. If you do not have a Will, then this is the time to think about who will get your property in the state of your new residence.

This is especially important for those who are married. The right of a spouse to inherit property varies significantly from state to state. There is a world of difference between the rights of a spouse in a community property state (Arizona, California, Idaho, Louisiana, New Mexico, Nevada, Texas, Washington and Wisconsin) and other states. There is even variation in the rights of a spouse from one community property state to another!

BURIAL PROVISIONS

If you own a burial site in Florida, you need to notify the cemetery of your change of address. It is important to notify them of your change of address, even if you move to a new location within the state. As discussed in Chapter 8, under Florida law, a burial site may be considered as abandoned after 50 years, unless the cemetery is able to locate the owner of that site (FS 497.353).

TAX CONSIDERATIONS

You need to check out the taxes of the new state. Each state has its own tax structure. Some states have an inheritance tax, or a transfer tax on inherited property. If state taxes are high, you may need an Estate Plan that will minimize the impact of those taxes.

CREDITOR PROTECTION

Creditor protection is another item that is significantly different state to state. Florida is known as "Debtor's Haven" because there are so many items that you can own free from the reach of your creditors, not the least of which is your homestead — regardless of its value. Many other states have virtually no creditor protection. In such states, anything you own can be taken by your creditors, in the event that you default in payment of monies owed. If you have much debt, then before moving to another state, check out what items are "creditor proof" in that state. Also determine what items can be inherited by your family free of your debts.

OTHER ESTATE PLANNING DOCUMENTS

Many states have laws directing physicians to honor a Medical Directive, such as a Living Will, that is properly drafted in another state. Other states will not recognize a Medical Directive unless it is drafted according to the laws of that state. But even if the laws of the state honor your Living Will or Designation of Health Care Surrogate, consider drafting a Medical Directive that conforms to the state of your new residence. Medical Directives vary significantly state to state. Other states may have laws that enable you to appoint someone with powers similar to a Health Care Surrogate, but the laws of the state may refer to such person as a *Patient Advocate* or a *Health Care Representative* or a *Health Care Agent.*

It is best to sign a new document using the form and terminology recognized in the new state, rather than chance any confusion should you become ill and find yourself in an emergency situation.

Similarly, if you have appointed someone to handle your finances under a Power of Attorney, you may want to have another prepared in conformity with the laws of the new state, so there will be no question of the right of your Agent to conduct business on your behalf.

RELOCATING THE MEDICAID RECIPIENT

If a family member is a Medicaid recipient, and you plan to move him to another state, you need to check whether he will continue to be eligible for Medicaid in that state. As explained in the previous chapter, Medicaid is both a state and federal program. Once a person qualifies for Medicaid in one state, he can be transferred to another state; provided he qualifies under that state's Medical Assistance program.

For example, Florida allows Spousal Refusal, but many other states do not. In such states the Applicant will be denied Medicaid benefits if the assets of the Community Spouse exceed the Resource limit for that state. If you plan to move a Medicaid Recipient to another state, it is important to first check with an Elder Law attorney in that state. He will explain the Medicaid eligibility laws of the state to you. He will be able to tell you what can be done in order to have the Recipient qualify for Medicaid in that state.

As you can see, state law has an important impact on your Estate Plan. When moving to another state you need to educate yourself about the laws of the state, or consult with an attorney who can assist you in reviewing your Estate Plan to see if that plan will accomplish your goals in that state.

✍ A SIGNIFICANT CHANGE IN THE LAW

We pay our legislators (state and federal) to make laws and, if necessary, change those in effect. We pay judges to interpret the law and that interpretation may change the way the law operates. The legislature and the judiciary do their job and so laws change frequently. Tax laws are particularly volatile. The 2001 change in the federal Estate Tax law gradually increases the Exclusion amount so that by 2010 no federal Estate Tax will be due regardless of the value of your Estate. You may be thinking that there is no need for an Estate Tax plan because you don't intend to die prior to 2010. But any certainty relating to death and taxes is false security (especially taxes, in this case). As explained in Chapter 2, the law as passed in 2001, is effective only until December 31, 2010. If lawmakers do nothing, then on January 1, 2011, the Federal Estate Tax goes back into effect; and Estates that exceed one million dollars will once again be subject to Estate taxes.

And that is not the only uncertainty. Each state has its own Estate Tax structure. It remains to be seen how each state will react to the federal change. Some states may follow the lead of the federal government and increase their Estate Tax Exclusion in the same manner. Other states may see this as an opportunity to "pick up the slack" i.e., to increase their Estate Taxes, so that monies that would have been paid to the federal government will now be paid to the state.

You need to keep up with the news to learn about changes in the law that affect your Estate Plan. It is a good idea to check with your attorney on a regular basis to see if any change in the state or federal law affects your current Estate plan. And also check out the Eagle Publishing Company Web site for changes we will post to keep this book fresh.   http://www.eaglepublishing.com

SPRING CLEAN YOUR RECORDS

Used to be, that housewives did a once a year, floor to ceiling, "spring housecleaning." We know of no survey telling whether today's houseperson conducts an annual purge of dirt and clutter. We suspect it went by the wayside when housewives entered the work force as full time employees. But it was a good practice. In many cases, it was the only time of the year when the house was truly clean and tidy. It is a good idea to incorporate that old-fashioned housecleaning practice to your financial records and clean them up on a regular basis. There is no need to keep the deed to real property that you have long since sold; a lease agreement to an apartment you no longer rent; a credit card to a closed account, etc.

Many hesitate to toss out some scrap of paper for fear it will not be available for future reference. There are documents you may need to keep for a lengthy period of time to establish a basis for tax purposes. You can avoid the problem of keeping too much, or not enough, by taking your box (or folder) of records with you the next time you visit with your accountant or attorney. You can ask your advisor to help you organize your records and assist with your "housecleaning."

Keys are another item to keep up to date. You may have a sentimental reason to keep old keys, but there is no business reason to keep a key to a car you no longer own, a safe deposit box you no longer lease, etc. Keeping such keys can only cause confusion should you become disabled or die. Whoever takes possession of your property will be left with mysterious keys. He will probably think the keys are protecting something of value.

Unless you enjoy picturing an heir's frustration as he seeks an imaginary treasure, pitch the key.

Glossary

ABSTRACT OF TITLE An *Abstract of Title* is a condensed history of the title to the land, consisting of a summary of all of documents recorded with the Clerk of the Circuit Court that affect the land, including mortgages.

ACTUARIAL TABLE An *actuarial table* is a table organized according to statistical data that indicates the life expectancy of a person.

ADDENDUM An *addendum* to a contract is an addition to the contract.

ADMINISTRATION The *administration* of a Probate Estate is the management and settlement of the decedent's affairs. There are different types of administration. See SUMMARY ADMINISTRATION.

ADMINISTRATIVE LAW JUDGE An *Administrative Law Judge* is someone who is appointed to conduct an administrative hearing. He has the power to administer oaths, take testimony, and then decide the facts of the case. Although he can decide the facts of the case, the final outcome of the hearing is decided by the government agency that appointed the Administrative Law Judge.

ADMINISTRATIVE CODE The *Administrative Code* is the set of rules used by governmental agencies to apply laws enacted by the legislature. The Administrative Code interprets the law and describes the agency's requirements to implement that law. See *CFR*.

AFFIANT An *Affiant* is someone who signs an affidavit and swears or acknowledges that it is true in the presence of a notary public or other person with authority to administer an oath or take acknowledgments.

AFFIDAVIT   An *Affidavit* is a written statement of fact made by someone voluntarily, under oath, or acknowledged as being true, in the presence of a notary public or someone else who has authority to administer an oath or take acknowledgments.

AGENT   An *Agent* is someone who is authorized by another (the principal) to act for or in place of the principal.

AGENCY ACCOUNT   An *Agency account* is a bank account in which the owner of the funds in the account authorizes another to make bank transactions as his Agent under a Power of Attorney.

AMENDMENT   An *amendment* to a Trust is an addition to the Trust that changes the provisions of the Trust.

ANATOMICAL GIFT   An *anatomical gift* is the donation of all or part of the body of the decedent for a specified purpose, such as transplantation or research.

ANNUAL GIFT TAX EXCLUSION   The *Annual Gift Tax Exclusion* is the amount a person can gift to another each year without being required to file a federal Gift Tax Return. The Annual Gift Tax Exclusion is currently $11,000.

ANNUITANT   An *Annuitant* is someone who is entitled to receive payments under an annuity contract.

ANNUITY CONTRACT An *annuity contract* is a contract that gives someone (the annuitant) the right to receive periodic payments (monthly, quarterly) for the life of the annuitant or for a given number of years.

ASSET An *asset* is anything owned by someone that has a value, including personal property (jewelry, paintings, securities, cash, motor vehicles, etc.) and real property (condominiums, vacant lots, acreage, residences, etc.).

ASSIGN To *assign* is to transfer one's rights to another; e.g. a person who has the right to receive income from a partnership may assign that right to another person,

ATTORNEY or ATTORNEY AT LAW An *attorney*, also known as an *Attorney at law*, or a *lawyer*, is someone who is licensed by the state to practice law in that state.

ATTORNEY-IN-FACT An *Attorney-In-Fact* is someone appointed to act as an Agent for another (the Principal) under a Power of Attorney.

AUGMENTED ESTATE In Florida, the *Augmented Estate* is the decedent's Estate less funeral and administrative expenses, and valid claims. It includes non Probate transfers, and gifts made by the decedent in excess of $3,000 made within 2 years of his death.

BASIS The *basis* is a value that is assigned to an asset for the purpose of determining the gain (or loss) on the sale of the item or in determining the value of the item in the hands of someone who has received it as a gift.

BENEFICIARY A *beneficiary* is one who benefits from the act of another or from the transfer of property. In this book we refer to a beneficiary as someone named in a Will, Trust, or deed to receive property, or someone who inherits property under the Laws of Intestate Succession.

BENEFICIARY ACCOUNT A *beneficiary account* is a bank account with a named beneficiary. The owner of the funds in the account directs the bank to give the funds remaining in the account to the named beneficiary upon the death of all of the owners of the bank account. Pay-On-Death and In-Trust-For accounts are beneficiary accounts.

BONA FIDE A *bona fide* act is something that is done in good faith; honestly, openly and without deceit or fraud.

BURDEN OF PROOF The *burden of proof* is the duty of one of the parties in a dispute to establish the facts in the case. Who has the burden of proof is established by law.

CAPITAL GAINS TAX A *Capital Gains Tax* is a tax on the increase in the basis of property sold by a taxpayer.

CASH SURRENDER VALUE The *Cash Surrender Value* of a life insurance policy is the amount of money the insurance company will pay to the owner of an insurance policy in the event the owner cancels the policy before the death of the person who is insured under the policy.

CFR   The *Code of Federal Regulations ("CFR")* is the annual cumulation of regulations set by federal executive agencies combined with previous regulations that are still in effect. The CFR contains the general body of laws that govern the practices and procedures of federal administrative agencies.

CHARITABLE REMAINDER ANNUITY TRUST A *Charitable Remainder Annuity Trust* is a Trust that pays an annuity to a designated person (the Annuitant) for a certain period of time or until his death. Once the annuity is paid, whatever remains in the Trust is donated to a tax exempt charity.

CIRCUIT A *Circuit* is a judicial division. The state of Florida is divided into 20 judicial circuits each with its own *Circuit Court*. Each judicial circuit covers one or more county.

CLAIM A *claim* against the decedent's Estate is a demand for payment. To be effective, the claim must be filed with the Probate court within the time limits set by law.

CLOSE CORPORATION A *Close Corporation* is a corporation whose voting shares are held by a single shareholder or a small, private, group of shareholders.

CODE A *Code* is a body of laws arranged systematically for easy reference e.g. the Internal Revenue Code.

CODICIL A *codicil* to a Will is an addition to the Will that changes or replaces certain parts of the Will.

COLUMBARIUM A *columbarium* is a vault with niches (spaces) for urns that contain the ashes of cremated bodies.

COMMON LAW MARRIAGE A *Common Law marriage* is one that is entered into without a state marriage license or any kind of official marriage ceremony. A Common Law marriage is created by an agreement to marry, followed by the two living together, and telling everyone they know that they are husband and wife. Florida does not recognize a Common Law marriage unless it was entered into in another state that considers the union to be a valid marriage.

COMMUNITY PROPERTY   Certain states (Arizona, California, Idaho, Louisiana, Nevada, New Mexico, Texas, Washington, and Wisconsin) have laws stating that property acquired by husband or wife, or both, during their marriage is *Community Property* and is owned equally by both of them.

CONFLICT OF INTEREST A *conflict of interest* is a conflict between the official duties of a fiduciary (guardian, Trustee, attorney, etc.) and his own private interest. For example, it is a conflict of interest for a Successor Trustee to use Trust property for his own personal profit.

CONSERVATOR A *Conservator* is someone appointed by the Probate Court to manage, protect and preserve the property of someone who is missing, or who the Court finds is unable to care for his property because of age (a minor) or incapacity.

CORPORATION   A *Corporation* is a company created by one or more persons according to the laws of the state. The company is owned by the *shareholders* or *stockholders*. Each owner has limited liability (see Limited Liability).

COURT The *Court* as used in this book is the Court that handles Probate matters. In Florida, the Probate Court is a department of the Circuit Court. When referring to an order made by the Court then the term is synonymous with "judge," i.e., an "order of the Court" is an order made by the judge of the Court.

CREDITOR A *creditor* is someone to whom a debt is owed by another person (the *debtor*).

CUSTODIAN A *Custodian* under the *Florida Uniform Gifts To Minors Act* is a person or financial institution who accepts responsibility for the care and management of property given to a minor child.

DEBTOR A *debtor* is someone who owes payment of money or services to another person (the *creditor*).

DECEDENT   The *decedent* is the person who died.

DESCENDANT   A *descendant* is someone who descends from a common ancestor. There are two kinds of descendants: a *lineal descendant* and a *collateral descendant*. The lineal descendant is one who descends in a straight line such as father to son to grandson. The collateral descendant is one who descends in a parallel line, such as a cousin. In this book, unless otherwise stated, the term *descendant* refers to a *lineal descendant*. The word **issue** has the same meaning as the word descendant.

DISTRIBUTION The *distribution* of a Trust or Probate Estate is the giving to the beneficiary that part of the Estate to which the beneficiary is entitled.

DURABLE As used in the Power of Attorney, the word *durable* means that the Power of Attorney will remain in effect in the event that the principal (the person giving the Power of Attorney) becomes incapacitated.

DURESS *Duress* is the use of force or threats to get someone to do something.

ELECTIVE SHARE The *Elective Share* is the minimum amount of the decedent's Estate that a surviving spouse is entitled to receive under law. In Florida that amount is one third of the decedent's *Augmented Estate*.

ENTITLEMENT An *entitlement* is a legal right to receive a benefit of income, property or services.

EQUITY The *equity* in a home is the market value of the home less monies owed on the property (mortgages, tax liens, etc.)

EQUITY INTEREST   An *equity interest* is an ownership interest. It is the value of the ownership interest over and above monies owed on the property.

ESS is the abbreviation for ***Economic Self-Sufficiency Specialist*** the member of the Florida Department of Children and Family Services who investigates whether an Applicant is qualified for Medicaid.

ESTATE A person's ***Estate*** is all of the property (both real and personal property) owned by that person. A person's Estate is also referred to as his ***Taxable Estate*** because all of the decedent's assets must be included when determining whether any Estate taxes are due when the person dies. Compare to ***Probate Estate***.

EXECUTOR An ***Executor***, or the feminine *Executrix*, are legal terms found in many Wills. The term refers to the person named by the Will maker to carry out directions given in the Will. Once a Court appoints the Executor for that job, he is referred to as the *Personal Representative*.

FACE VALUE The *face value* of a life insurance policy is the value stated on the insurance certificate or policy. It is the amount to be paid upon the death of the insured person.

FAIR HEARING A ***Fair Hearing*** is an administrative procedure. In Florida, it is conducted by the Department of Children and Family Services. It is the first step in the appeals process for someone who has been denied Medicaid benefits.

FIDUCIARY A ***Fiduciary*** is one who takes on the duty of holding property in Trust for another or acting for the benefit of another, such as a Personal Representative, Trustee, Guardian etc.. A fiduciary relationship is also one that is developed out of trust and confidence. For example, an attorney has a fiduciary relationship with his client.

GRANTEE The *Grantee* of a deed (also called the party of the second part) named in a deed is the person who receives title to the property from the grantor.

GRANTOR A *Grantor* is someone who transfers property. The Grantor of a deed (also called the party of the first part), is the person who transfers property to a new owner (the *Grantee*). The Grantor of a Trust is someone who creates the Trust and then transfers property into the Trust. Also see *Settlor*.

GUARANTOR A *Guarantor* is someone who promises to pay a debt or perform a contract for another in the event that person does not fulfill his obligation.

GUARDIAN A *Guardian* is someone who has legal authority to care for the person or property of a minor or for someone who has been found by the court to be incapacitated.

HEALTH CARE ADVANCE DIRECTIVE A *Health Care Advance Directive* is a writing made by someone (the *Declarant*) according to Florida law in which the Declarant gives directions about the health care he wishes to receive in the event that he is too ill to speak for himself. The Health Care Advance Directive can include a *Designation of Health Care Surrogate* and *Living Will* or both.

HEALTH CARE SURROGATE A *Health Care Surrogate* is some-one appointed by another (the Declarant) to make medical decisions for the Declarant in the event he is too ill to speak for himself.

HEIR An *heir* is someone who is entitled to inherit the decedent's property in the event that the decedent dies without a Will. This includes the surviving spouse as well as the state of Florida, if the decedent had no surviving relative.

HOMESTEAD The *homestead* is the dwelling that is owned, and occupied, in the state of Florida, as the owner's principal residence.

INCAPACITATED The term *incapacitated* is used in two ways. A person is *physically incapacitated* if he lacks the ability to perform certain tasks, or care for himself in some way. A person is *legally incapacitated* if a Court finds that he is unable to care for his person or property.

INTER VIVOS TRUST An *Inter Vivos Trust* (also known as a *Revocable Living Trust*) is a Trust that is created and becomes effective during the lifetime of the Settlor (or Grantor). A *revocable* Trust is one which can be amended or revoked by the Grantor or Settlor during his lifetime.

IRREVOCABLE CONTRACT An *irrevocable contract* is a contract that cannot be revoked, withdrawn, or cancelled by any of the parties to that contract.

IRREVOCABLE TRUST An *Irrevocable Trust* is a Trust that cannot be cancelled or terminated until its purpose is accomplished.

IRREVOCABLE INSURANCE TRUST An *Irrevocable Insurance Trust* is a Trust that is set up to purchase life insurance. The proceeds of the life insurance policy can be used to pay taxes that may be due upon the death of the insured person.

ISSUE The decedent's *issue* are his descendants, children, grandchildren, great-grandchildren, etc. See DESCENDANT.

IRA ACCOUNT An *Individual Retirement Account ("IRA")* is a retirement savings account in which income taxes on certain deposits and interest to the account are deferred until the monies are withdrawn from the account.

JOINT AND SEVERAL LIABILITY If two or more people agree to be *jointly and severally liable* to pay a debt, then each individually agrees to be responsible to pay the debt, and together they all agree to pay for the debt.

JOINT TENANCY WITH RIGHT OF SURVIVOR In Florida, a *Joint Tenancy with right of survivor* means that each tenant owns an equal share of the property. Should one Joint Tenant die the remaining tenants own the property.

KEOGH PLAN A *Keogh Plan* is a retirement plan available to self-employed taxpayers. Certain tax benefits are available such as tax deductions for annual contributions to the plan. The plan is named for its author, Eugene James Keogh.

KEY MAN INSURANCE *Key man insurance* is a disability and life insurance policy designed to protect a company from economic loss in the event that an important employee of the company becomes disabled or dies.

LAWS OF INTESTATE SUCCESSION The *Laws of Intestate Succession* are the laws of the state that determine who is to inherit the decedent's Probate Estate if the decedent died without a valid Will.

LEGALESE   *Legalese* refers to the use of legal terms and confusing text used by some attorneys when drafting legal documents.

LETTERS *Letters* is a document, issued by the Probate court, giving the Personal Representative authority to take possession of and to administer the Estate of the decedent.

LIEN   A *lien* is a charge against a person's property as security for a debt. The lien is evidence of the creditor's right to take the property as full or partial payment, in the event that the debtor defaults in paying the monies owed.

LIFE ESTATE A *Life Estate* interest in real property is the right to possess and receive the income from that property for so long as the holder of the Life Estate lives. A one-third Life Estate interest means the person can occupy one-third of the property or receive one-third of the income generated by that property.

LIMITED LIABILITY *Limited Liability,* as related to a corporation or other company created according to state law, means that a shareholder of the company generally is not responsible to pay the debts of the company beyond the amount that he/she invested in the company.

LIMITED LIABILITY COMPANY A *Limited Liability Company* is a company created according to the laws of the state, to conduct business or for any other lawful purpose. All of the members of the company have limited liability.

LIMITED PARTNERSHIP A *Limited Partnership* is a partnership created according to the laws of the state. Each *Limited Partner* has limited liability. Each *General Partner* has control of the business and is personally liable for all of the debts of the company. (See Limited Liability).

LINEAL DESCENDANT See *descendant.*

LITIGATION *Litigation* is the process of carrying on a lawsuit, i.e., to sue for some right or remedy in a court of law. A Litigation Attorney is one who is experienced in conducting the law suit and in particular, going to trial.

LIVING WILL A *Living Will* is a Health Care Advance Directive that gives instructions to the physician about whether life support systems should be withheld or withdrawn in the event that the person who signs the Living Will (the "Declarant") is terminally ill or in a persistent vegetative state and unable to speak for himself.

LOOK-BACK PERIOD The *Look-back Period* is a period of consecutive months that can be reviewed for transfers of Resources to determine whether a period of ineligibility should be imposed for the Medicaid Applicant.

MEDICAID *Medicaid* is a medical assistance program sponsored jointly by the federal and state government to provide health care for people with low income and limited resources. In many states, the program is also referred to as *Medical Assistance.*

NET WORTH A person's *net worth* is the value of all of the property that he owns less what he owes.

NEXT OF KIN *Next of kin* has two meanings in law: *next of kin* refers to a person's nearest blood relation or it can refer to those people (not necessarily blood relations) who are entitled to inherit the property of a person who dies without a valid Will.

NON-PROBATE TRANSFER A *Non-Probate Transfer* is a transfer made to a beneficiary of the decedent without going through a Probate procedure. This includes transfers from a joint account, a Trust, a Pay-On-Death account, a Transfer-On-Death security, etc.

PARTNERSHIP A business *partnership* is an agreement between two or more persons to use their assets and/or services to carry on a business for profit as co-owners.

PERSONAL EFFECTS *Personal effects* is personal property that is kept for one's personal use such as clothing, jewelry, books, and other items generally found in the home.

PERSONAL PROPERTY *Personal property* is all property owned by a person that is not real property (real estate). It includes personal effects, cars, securities, bank accounts, insurance policies, etc.

PERSONAL REPRESENTATIVE The *Personal Representative* is someone appointed by the Surrogate's Court to settle the decedent's Estate and to distribute whatever is left to the proper beneficiary.

PER STIRPES *Per Stirpes* is a method of distributing property to a group of beneficiaries such that if one of them dies before the gift is made, the deceased person's share goes to his/her descendants. If there are no descendants, then the surviving beneficiaries divide the property equally among themselves.

PETITION A *Petition* is a formal written, request to a Court asking the Court to take action or issue an order on a given matter; e.g. a request to appoint a Guardian.

POSTNUPTIAL AGREEMENT A *Postnuptial agreement* is an Agreement made by a couple after marriage to decide their respective rights in case of a dissolution or the death of a spouse.

POWER OF ATTORNEY A *Power of Attorney* is a document in which someone (the *Principal*) gives another (his *Agent*) authority to do specific things on behalf of the Principal.

PRENUPTIAL AGREEMENT A *Prenuptial Agreement* (also known as an *Antenuptial Agreement*) is an agreement made prior to marriage whereby a couple determines how their property is to be managed during their marriage and how their property is to be divided should either die, or they later divorce.

PRINCIPAL OF A POWER OF ATTORNEY The *Principal* of a Power of Attorney is someone who gives another (his *Agent*) authority to act on his (the Principal's) behalf.

PRINCIPAL OF A TRUST   The *Principal* of a Trust is the Trust property. The Trust income is the monies that are earned on the Trust Principal.

PROBABLE CAUSE   *Probable cause* exists if it is reasonable to believe certain facts. Mere suspicion is not enough. For probable cause to exist, there must be more evidence for the facts than against.

PROBATE   *Probate* is a Court procedure in which a Court determines the existence of a valid Will. The Decedent's Estate is settled by the Personal Representative who pays all valid claims and then distributes whatever remains to the proper beneficiary.

PROBATE ESTATE The *Probate Estate* is that part of the decedent's Estate that is subject to a Probate procedure. It includes property that the decedent owned in his name only. It does not include property that was jointly held by the decedent and someone else. It does not include property held "in trust for" or "for the benefit of" someone.

PRO BONO The term *Pro Bono* means "for the public good." When an attorney works Pro Bono, he does so voluntarily and without pay.

REAL PROPERTY   *Real property,* also known as *real estate,* is land and anything permanently attached to the land such as buildings and fences.

REMAINDER INTEREST   A *Remainder Interest* in real property is the property that passes to a beneficiary at the end of the life interest i.e. the property that passes to the beneficiary once the owner of the Life Estate dies.

RESIDUARY BENEFICIARY A *residuary beneficiary* of a Will is a beneficiary who is entitled to whatever is left of the Probate Estate once the specific gifts made in the Will have been distributed and once the decedent's bills, taxes and costs of Probate have been paid. If there is more than one residuary beneficiary, then they all share equally in the residuary Estate, unless the Will provides for a different distribution.

RESOURCE A *Resource* for purposes of determining Medicaid eligibility, is an asset owned by the decedent, or his spouse, that can be converted to meet their needs. Federal statute 42 U.S.C. 1382b identifies what is (and is not) counted as a Resource.

REVOCABLE TRUST   A *Revocable Trust* is a Trust which can be amended or revoked by the Grantor or Settlor during his lifetime.

REVOCABLE LIVING TRUST A *Revocable Living Trust* (also known as an *Inter Vivos Trust*) is a Revocable Trust that is created and becomes effective during the lifetime of the Grantor or Settlor.

SELF PROVED WILL A *Self Proved Will* is a Will that eliminates some of the formalities of proof in a Probate procedure. The Will is made Self Proved by an Affidavit, signed by the witnesses, in the form as required by the statute.

SETTLOR A *Settlor* or a *Trustor* is someone who creates a Trust.

SIBLING   A *sibling* is one of two or more people born of the same parents; i.e., a brother or a sister. Unless, otherwise noted, we used the term to include those who have only one parent in common; i.e. a half brother or a half sister.

SOLE PROPRIETORSHIP A *Sole Proprietorship* is a form of business ownership in which one person owns all of the assets of the business and that person is personally liable for all of the debts of the business.

SOLEMNIZE To *solemnize* a marriage is to enter into a marriage publicly, before witnesses, in contrast to a secretive or common law marriage.

SPECIFIC GIFT   A *Specific Gift* is a gift of a specific item of the Will maker's Estate that is made to a named beneficiary of the Will.

SPENDTHRIFT   A *Spendthrift* is someone who wastes money and/or spends lavishly.

SPENDTHRIFT TRUST   A *Spendthrift Trust* is a Trust created to provide monies for the living expenses of a beneficiary, and at the same time protect the monies from being taken by the creditors of the beneficiary.

STANDBY GUARDIAN A *Standby Guardian* is someone appointed by a parent to take over the care of a child in the event that the parent becomes incapacitated or dies.

STATUTE OF LIMITATION A *Statute of Limitation* is a federal or state law that sets maximum time periods for taking legal action. Once the time set out in the statute passes, no legal action can be taken.

STEPPED-UP BASIS   A *stepped-up basis* is the value placed on property that is acquired in a taxable transaction such as inheriting property or purchasing property (Internal Revenue Code 1012). The "step-up" refers to the increase in value from the basis of the former owner (usually what he paid for it), to the basis of the new owner (usually the market value when the transfer is made).

SUCCESSOR TRUSTEE   A *Successor Trustee* is someone who takes the place of the Trustee.

SUMMARY ADMINISTRATION A *Summary Administration* is a simplified and/or shortened Probate procedure.

SURROGATE A *Surrogate* is a substitute; someone who acts in place of another. A *Health Care Surrogate* is someone who is appointed by another (the Declarant) to make medical decisions for the Declarant in the event he is too ill to speak for himself.

TENANCY BY THE ENTIRETY A *Tenancy by the Entirety* is the name of a form of ownership of real property held by a husband and wife. It is a joint tenancy with right of survivorship, modified by the common law theory that the husband and wife are one. With a joint tenancy with right of survivor, each joint tenant owns their own share of the property until death, when the surviving owner owns it 100%. With a Tenancy by the Entirety, each owns 100% of the property both before and after death.

TENANCY IN COMMON *Tenancy In Common* is a form of ownership such that each tenant owns his/her share without any claim to that share by the other tenants. Unlike a joint tenancy, there is no right of survivorship. Once a tenant in common dies, his/her share belongs to the tenant's Estate and not to the remaining owners of the property.

TERM LIFE INSURANCE POLICY A *Term Life Insurance policy* insures the life of a person for a certain period of time. No insurance proceeds are paid unless the insured person dies within the given period of time. The monies paid for the policy are not refundable, so a Term Life Insurance policy has no cash surrender value.

TITLE INSURANCE *Title Insurance* is a policy issued by a title company after searching title to the property. The insurance covers losses that result from a defect of title, such as unpaid taxes, or someone with a claim of ownership of the property.

TRUST AGREEMENT A *Trust agreement* is a document in which someone (the Grantor or Settlor) creates a Trust and appoints a Trustee to manage property placed into the Trust. The usual purpose of the Trust is to benefit persons or charities named by the Grantor as beneficiaries of the Trust.

TRUSTEE   A *Trustee* is a person, or institution, who accepts the duty of caring for property for the benefit of another.

UNASSIGNABLE ANNUITY An *unassignable annuity* is an annuity that cannot be assigned; i.e., the annuitant's benefits cannot be transferred to another.

UNDUE INFLUENCE   *Undue influence* is pressure, influence or persuasion that overpowers a person's free will or judgment, so that a person acts according to the will or purpose of the dominating party.

VOID PROVISION A *void provision* is one that is not legally enforceable. For example, if a Will provision makes a gift and the Court finds that provision to be void, then the beneficiary has no legal right to receive that gift.

WAIVER   A *waiver* is the intentional and voluntary giving up of a known right.

INDEX

211 Florida Statutes and Regulations are referenced in
A Will Is Not Enough In Florida

Each state has its own set of laws relating to the control, and protection of a person's Estate. The laws of STATE relating to Guardianship, Probate and especially Medicaid are very different from the laws of other states.

The author is in the process of "translating" *A Will Is Not Enough* for the rest of the states; that is, writing state specific books that explain how to set up an Estate Plan for the given state and how to qualify for MEDICAID in that state.

A Will Is Not Enough is now available for:
ARIZONA, CALIFORNIA, CONNECTICUT, COLORADO
FLORIDA, HAWAII, INDIANA, MARYLAND
MICHIGAN, MASSACHUSETTS, NEBRASKA
NEW JERSEY, NEW MEXICO, NEW YORK,
OREGON, PENNSYLVANIA, TEXAS
VIRGINIA, WASHINGTON, WISCONSIN.

To check whether this book is currently available for other states call Eagle Publishing Company of Boca at
(800) 824-0823
or visit our Web site http://www.eaglepublishing.com

**SPECIAL OFFER FOR PURCHASERS OF THIS BOOK
$25 INCLUDES SHIPPING**

How To Defend Yourself Against Your Lawyer

is a book about the unhappy experiences people have with their lawyers, beginning with that of the author AMELIA E. POHL. She became involved in a law suit and was surprised at how many times she had been misled by attorneys who were supposed to be on her side. She wondered if she, a lawyer, could be taken, what chance does a person with no legal background have? This book is a result of those concerns.

The book is divided into chapters that cover the most common problems that take people to a lawyer: divorce, wills, probate, criminal, personal injury, starting a business, buying a house, etc. Each chapter contains an interesting short story about a person's experience when they hired a lawyer for that given area of law. Each chapter explains how to find "Mr. Right Lawyer" for the job, and what to do, if you employed "Mr. Wrong." This book is an interesting read even for those who have no present legal problem, but if the reader ever finds the need for a lawyer, he will be glad he read this book.

Copyright 2004   272 pages   6" X 9" soft cover
$20 includes Shipping and Handling

Beyond Grief To Acceptance and Peace

AMELIA E. POHL and the noted psychologist BARBARA J. SIMMONDS, Ph.d, have written a book for those families who have suffered a loss.

What to say to the bereaved

❖ How to help a child through the loss

❖ Strategies to adjust to a new life-style

❖ When and where to seek assistance.

80 pages   6" X 9" $10 includes Shipping and Handling

Guiding Those Left Behind

Amelia E. Pohl has written a series of books explaining how to settle an Estate. Each book is state specific, telling how things are done in that state. Each book explains:

⬦ who to notify

⬦ how to locate the decedent's property

⬦ how to get possession of the inheritance

⬦ when you do, and do not, need an attorney

⬦ the rights of a beneficiary, and much more.

Each book is written with the assistance of an experienced attorney who is licensed and is practicing in that state.

The *Guiding* series is currently available for the following states: ALABAMA, ARIZONA, CALIFORNIA, CONNECTICUT
FLORIDA, GEORGIA, HAWAII, FLORIDA, INDIANA
IOWA, KENTUCKY, LOUISIANA, MASSACHUSETTS
MARYLAND, MICHIGAN, MINNESOTA, MISSOURI
MISSISSIPPI, NEW JERSEY, NEW YORK
NORTH CAROLINA, OHIO, OKLAHOMA
PENNSYLVANIA, SOUTH CAROLINA, TENNESSEE
TEXAS, UTAH, VIRGINIA, WASHINGTON, WISCONSIN

Visit our Web site http://www.eaglepublishing.com
to check whether books for other states are available at this time.

SPECIAL OFFER FOR PURCHASERS OF THIS BOOK
$22 INCLUDES SHIPPING

To order call (800) 824-0823

It is the goal of EAGLE PUBLISHING COMPANY to keep our publications fresh.

As we receive information about changes to the federal or Florida law we will post an update to this edition at our Web site:

http://www.eaglepublishing.com